Mess

to

Message

Perspective and Encouragement to Help You Focus Forward

Scott Wittig

Allison T. Cain

Mess to Message
Written by Scott Wittig & Allison T. Cain
Cover Design by Kent Swecker
Photography: Fran Dickenson (Allison T. Cain)

Scripture quotations from the English Standard Version Study Bible, Copyright
2008 © by Good News Publishers

Scripture quotations are from the Holy Bible, New International Version,
copyright © 1973, 1978, 1984 by International Bible Society.

Scripture quotations are from Reading God's Story, A Chronological Daily Bible
(HCSB), copyright © 1999, 2000, 2002, 2003, 2009 by Holman Bible Publishers.

Scripture quotations from THE MESSAGE. Copyright © 1993, 1994, 1995,
1996, 2000, 2001, 2002. Used by permission of NavPress Publishing Group.

Scott Wittig - scott@scottwittig.com
Allison T. Cain - atcain2@earthlink.net

ISBN-9781796641110

FIRST PRINTING

To order additional copies of this resource, visit www.scottwittig.com,
www.allisonTcain.com, or www.amazon.com.
Printed in the United States of America

This book is dedicated to the memory of our precious
little friend, Ella Newmiller, whose heroic fight against cancer
connected so many people including these two authors who really,
really enjoyed life alongside her.

And to all those mentioned in this book, and those who aren't,
we trust God has specifically woven you into our lives. We honor how
you have helped make us who we are today.

CONTENTS

Mess To Message

FORWARD

By Owen Barrow
   Pastor, 519 Church

When people are feeling their way through the roughest moments of their lives, no matter how great or how minor, the first thing I always do is listen intently to their stories. There is no greater way to honor the experience of another than to hear them out. I ask questions. I try to understand the depth and breadth of their not-so-good moments before I ever offer any counsel.

As I listen to them, I am also listening out for the work and word of God in the middle of it all. When life gets noisy, it can become difficult to hear what God is saying to us, and so, I have the holy task of listening on their behalf. As some of my people say, "I have one ear listening out for them, and one ear listening out for the Holy Spirit."

Once their story is told and I get a chance to speak, I always seem to start off the same way. Not because I learned it in school, or cooked up some grand plan for pastoring on a mountaintop retreat. It just sort of happened this way.

"Well, first let me say…"

And then I get the privilege of speaking a word of grace, a word of hope, a word of identity, a word of belonging and purpose into the middle of their mess. Not my word, mind you. I get a chance to speak to them the word I heard on their behalf.

You may or may not be surprised to know that this is the greatest delight of my ministry. I speak each weekend publicly for about thirty minutes. I tell stories. We laugh. We lean in to hear what God might be trying to say in scripture. I teach. We learn. It is great. The preaching moment is a glorious thing, but nothing is better than the moment I get to stare someone in the eyes and let them know that God has not forgotten about them.

That is always the fear when not-so-good things happen in our lives—that God has forgotten about us. Listen to the poet wring his hands and tear his clothes in Psalm 13.

1 How long, O Lord? Will you forget me forever?
  How long will you hide your face from me?
2 How long must I bear pain in my soul,
  and have sorrow in my heart all day long?
How long shall my enemy be exalted over me?

God has not forgotten you. God has not hidden his face. Stand up straight and know that in spite of what it looks like around you, and in the midst of your mess that God is present. Join your voice with that same poet but a few verses later:

5 But I trusted in your steadfast love;
  my heart shall rejoice in your salvation.
6 I will sing to the Lord,
  because he has dealt bountifully with me.

For those of you in a not-so-good sort of moment or for anyone who has ever found themselves in the middle of a mess, this book is for you. It is an invitation for you to journey with a pair of guides who are unabashedly, freshly and authentically like the rest of us; a pair who are not perfect. And yet, it is not simply a reminder that we are all in this <u>together</u>, it is a reminder that we are not in this <u>alone</u> — that God is with us. Sometimes it is just easier to see Him in someone else's story. At the conclusion of each of Scott's stories, you will hear Allison stare you in the eye and speak a word of grace into your life so that you will know that God has not forgotten you.

May the fullness of God's blessings be with you as you journey through these pages with Scott and Allison.

INTRODUCTION

Fear not.
No, really, it is possible to have no fear. You just need perspective.

I have been granted an incredible amount of perspective in my forty-seven years on this planet. Forty-seven years filled with a lot of awesome—and a lot of trying—times. Writing about those trials and the trials of some people close to me coupled with reflection from my friend Allison after each chapter in this book has been part of an awakening for which I am incredibly thankful. Another part of this awakening came just after one of the most difficult times any of us can face—the mental deterioration and loss of a parent.

I remember where I was standing in the nursing home when my mother's doctor and I agreed that it was time to switch her to a treatment plan of comfort measures—it was at the nurse's station that sat between my mother's room and the cafeteria where I had just tried to feed her Thanksgiving Day meal to her. Her dementia had taken away the mother I had loved my whole life to the point where she could not remember to swallow the food I had just put in her mouth.

After fighting back my tears throughout the meal, I had wheeled my mom back to her room. During that walk to her room, I felt my emotions building up a pressure that simply had to be released. Barely into her room, I turned her wheelchair around so she was facing the hallway instead of into her room. I walked to her bed, grabbed a pillow, knelt down, buried my face in that pillow and wailed. The months of watching my mom fall away came to a crescendo that could've been heard miles away had my face not been buried on her bed.

I soon felt a hand rubbing my back. For a second I thought (and hoped) it was the hand of my mother. Instead, it was the hand that took care of my mother—our favorite nurse's assistant, Seree. I saw her big, beautiful, caring smile when I lifted my head just as *she* had seen *my* sad, upset, about-to-explode-with-emotions face when I had been trying to nourish my mother in the cafeteria just moments earlier. Seree and her kind-hearted, beautiful soul cared for my mom and me that day and on many of the days of the four months that followed that Thanksgiving Day; the four months it took before my mom was healed of dementia and taken to heaven. My mom became an angel, I believe, and that angel on earth named Seree who cared for her in her last days also went to my mother's service.

Just after the service, my brother and sister and I were walking past the serene lake that borders the cemetery in the woods where we buried both our parents within two years of each other. We were talking about our brother-sister relationships and what they may look like now that we had lost our parents. My brother stopped us in our tracks and said, "I have an idea—let's throw our sadness and fear in the lake." We paused for a second so our little brains could catch up with that big statement, then we threw our sadness and fear in the lake. The recovery and grieving process from losing my mother proved to be infinitely faster than it was after we buried my father in that beautiful place and I believe that wonderful activity my brother suggested is the reason. We let go of fear.

Years passed without me giving another thought to this, but then I found myself paralyzed while at church; not paralyzed with fear but paralyzed because I couldn't think of a fear. You will read later about a wonderful activity that Pastor Owen often asks us to do as a response to a sermon. On this day, a Sunday in January when the new sermon series "Year Without Fear" had been introduced, we were handed a sticky note and a pen and asked to write down a fear we would like to give away, to let go. Once written, we could stick it to the whiteboard at the front of the room and start the process of ridding ourselves of that fear. Pastor Owen had taken a seat right in front of me and was about to write his own fear, displaying a trait I have always loved about him—he participates right alongside us. I leaned forward and whispered, "Is it good, bad or indifferent that I can't come up with a single fear to write down?" His response was pretty awesome, literally, because he said, "Ummm…that's pretty awesome."

No fear? Really? Is this guy writing this book perfect or something?
You may be having those thoughts right now, and I get it.

However, my wife and kids will gladly give you examples of how this guy writing the book is NOT perfect. Not. Even. Close. I simply could not come up with a fear. How? Why?

I believe it is partly because of the exercise I did with my brother and sister on that warm April day at the cemetery, but it is mostly because of the perspective I have gotten from writing this book, reading Allison's response to each chapter and leaning on faith. My prayer is that you get the same perspective from immersing yourself in this book and can become fearless as well. If you can be a student of life just as I try to be, you will not only see but also believe that good can (and will) come from not-so-good; that there is a message to come from the mess. If you are as lucky as I am to find the intestinal fortitude and vulnerability to share that message with an audience, you will find yourself…

In a place where fear has no place in your life.

Where you have a positive outlook.

Where you find the good.

Where you—after reading Allison's responses to each chapter—can begin a relationship with God or find your way into a deeper, more trusting relationship with Him.

*

It would be predictable to write a book with such a ginormous mission as ours by sharing stories of people with ginormous names and celebrity. People who have "made it." Arrived. People with clout and personal assistants. NOPE! Not happenin' here. You are getting ready to hear about this Average Joe's mess and that of some of my friends. Every-day people. Every-day messes. This won't be, *How to Become a Millionaire in Six Seconds* but rather, *The Millionaire Next Door.* You may hear some stories about Scott, the short, bald guy done-good, but you will also hear about this little guy who woulda, coulda, shoulda done this or that in certain situations. I'm about as bashful about sharing stuff I've messed up as I am when it comes to joking about my shiny head or lack of vertical inches. If telling you a story about adopting a 100-pound, ten-year-old, arthritic, flea-ridden dog from an addict who was heading to rehab is going to help you in some way; you are getting ready to hear it. The good from the not-so-good—that's the theme here, friends.

My name is Scott, and I'll be your tour guide along with my dear friend Allison. In each chapter, you will find my story followed by a biblical reflection from Allison. We believe that owning the perspective that a message can come from a mess not only grants us strength and perspective to claw through the fight that our own life challenges pose but also the wisdom and words that our friends, family, and loved ones need as they seek our love and assistance during their battles. If you are living through some messiness of your own, find hope in these pages. Our prayer is that you will look back to this book as a force that led you toward good and God, like my friend Allen did for me.

ALLEN

Flipping a house leads to faith in God. Sounds like a provocative headline, but that is what happened a few years back.

I was about 15 years into the career that took all of my hair, the stressful life of a mortgage loan officer. Any successful person in this role will tell you that it is crucial to develop relationships with top local Realtors as they can be great referral partners. Having done this, my wife and I always faced a conundrum when it came time to buy or sell a house. How do I pick one of my referral partners without ticking off the others?

On one transaction, my friend and Realtor partner, Allen, made it easy for us—he brought us a listing for a house that could make us money as a flip. Jeanne and I had recently moved from the outskirts of Raleigh to a more populated area with amenities more nearby, a crucial feature in the life of parents of a two-year-old with a second child on the way. The home we purchased looked like an 800 square foot ranch. Looks were deceiving, though, because it had recently been completely renovated and updated, to include two wings off the back that created a U-shaped footprint made up of 3100 square feet. It was gorgeous. Part of the allure was that it was a flip for the person selling it so we would be the first owners to enjoy its newness. The mortgage business had been very good to us, and we felt the time was right to reward ourselves as our family grew.

Realtors: How to endear yourself to a friend and possible customer—put a potential windfall in front of them. Allen's timing was good since we were living in the fruits of a flipper's labor and had seen the numbers regarding how much the seller of the home we had just purchased had paid and how much he received after his hard work.

The house Allen put us in front of was a sure thing. It was a nice-looking ranch with a two-car garage on a wooded lot in a highly desirable neighborhood with great schools and in close proximity to major highways. The three bedrooms were all good sized and didn't need anything but new carpet and a fresh coat of paint. The two and a half bathrooms, on the other hand, needed some serious love. Bathrooms and kitchens sell houses, so we knew where our efforts needed to be focused.

This would be our first flip. We just needed to do like they do on TV, right? We would do a little bit of work with as minimal of an investment as possible and sell that sucker for a bunch more than we paid.

Yeah right.

A structural inspection revealed a host of issues, with the biggest being a sizeable crack in the foundation. Our perspective and project scope dramatically changed after we learned not only what *had* to be fixed but what a buyer of *this home in this area* was going to demand. This home, which was very close to our new home, was near enough to a highly coveted area of Raleigh that we would joke about being able to smell the food from over in *that* neighborhood. You don't get away with cutting corners in an area like that.

After many dollars spent and months passed, we got around to listing the house for sale so we could get our money out and maybe make a few bucks, but it didn't turn out to be the windfall we had hoped. As sellers of the property, we were required to complete a property disclosure alerting potential buyers about any known issues in the home. This is where I made it clear to Allen that I was a candidate for some proselytizing in the coming days. He wanted me to disclose it, and I didn't want to disclose it; the foundation crack that I felt like we had cured. Some experts had told me it was only cured by a $13,000 fix and others said otherwise, so "otherwise" it was. The minimum had been done, and I was keeping it to myself. I said something like, "Allen, let me ask you this—if you were selling a car and the back door didn't open and close perfectly…if you had to put a little shoulder into it to open the door, would you tell that to a buyer during the test drive?"

While I don't think anyone would say I was morally bankrupt, The Golden Rule was not front-and-center in my life *yet*, nor was I was looking to follow it in the sale of this home. Yes, there are omissions you can legally make when selling a home. What bugged Allen more than anything was that the dollars mattered more than the sense for me as a seller and, more importantly, as a person.

A few weeks after the home sold, Allen and I went to lunch. Afterward, I pulled into the parking lot of his real estate office to drop him off. As he got out of the car, he said, "Hang on, I need to grab something for you from my car." Was it a closing gift? A 'thank you' for the business we had just given him? *He ought to thank us. He made more than we did on that deal,* I thought. I was happy when he returned with a gift in hand, one for which I can never really thank him.

A few days after tucking the CD Allen had given me as a gift into the console of my SUV, I had some drive time with my dad. Forty-something years of fighting diabetes had taken its toll on his eyes, and he needed me to drive him to a surgical appointment an hour and a half from home. For so many years (my entire life), I had seen my dad deal with this disease without too much of an impact on his daily activities. He *would* occasionally have "insulin reactions" as he called them—episodes where his blood sugar would seem to fall off a cliff suddenly, and he'd have to suck on a bottle of glucose to get it back in balance. He fought those off with the same vigor that he had for virtually all tasks he took on, though. Outside of those tough moments, the most outward evidence of his battle was that we would see his boxer shorts every morning at breakfast and every evening at dinner because he gave himself a shot in the upper thigh and wasn't afraid to do it right there at the table!

After following me south from New York to North Carolina, I watched my father start to suffer from his years-long fight. The ultimate insult happened when, shortly after moving into a nationally recognized retirement community that housed two beautiful Robert Trent Jones golf courses, he found himself no longer able to hold a club in his hands; circulation issues took this ability away. Throughout my 30's, I witnessed his decline yet did my best to not point out my observations. Truly, there was no need to do so since they tended to manifest themselves in obvious ways through miscues and falls, mostly due to his declining vision. Diabetes proved later that it had taken a toll on his heart, but that muscle was, fortunately, still in good shape when I dropped this bomb on him on our car ride to eye surgery, "Dad, why didn't we go to church more when I was growing up?"

I kept my eyes on the road for many reasons, not the least of which was not wanting to see his anger build. Dad had a temper like a third rail, and I had touched it a number of times as I was coming up. I didn't have a clue where his head was on this subject and held my breath that church wasn't a third rail issue. I was thankful when anger didn't surface; it was instead replaced with an audible, long-awaited sigh of relief. I remember the sound to this day. My father had been provided with the moment to tell me why faith had not figured much in the life of our family, or at least why worship hadn't.

"Scotty, it was just too much. Your sister was such a handful with all of the problems she had—it was too much work to get us all to church every week. I know that's not the greatest answer, but that's what happened. We went when we could."

"So you and mom believe in God?"

"Yes, of course, we do."

Permission. While this conversation didn't explain to me why God was not in the discussion of our daily lives during my formative years, it told me that it's ok for *this* Wittig to believe. Now it was going to be up to me how I could make it part of <u>my</u> family's conversation going forward.

The gift Allen had given me was a CD called, *The Invitation,* narrated by Rick Warren, Saddleback Church pastor and author of *The Purpose Driven Life.* A few weeks after that precious time in the car with my dad (on the first listen…in my car…alone), I did what Rick Warren asked me to do when he spoke between songs; I accepted Jesus Christ as my Lord and Savior. I said 'yes' to this so easily because I needed to. The timing was right. I was ready. I had permission. When you're an adult, you don't find yourself needing permission to do much of anything anymore; you just do it. The readiness and permission to allow the Father into my life (where I'm sure He had been, but I didn't see Him) came from *my* father.

I was now part of "the club"—a club filled with really, really good people whose quest in life is to do the right thing and do right by others. Allen invited me into the club at just the right time; it turns out.

Mess to message: *A real estate deal, some questionable thinking on my part and the need for a ride to eye surgery opens the door to a relationship with God that I never saw coming. Thank you, Allen, for helping open that door. Ever since you gave me this gift I have paid close attention to the fact that your beliefs don't make you a better person, your behavior does.*

† YOU ARE PLAN A †

I wonder if Allen worried that sharing *The Invitation* CD with Scott would ruin their friendship? Did he make the conscious decision that an eternal friendship with Scott meant more than an earthly one? How long would it have taken Scott to seek the Lord and ask Him into his life and heart if Allen hadn't stepped up and in? How disappointed would God have been if Allen had ignored His nudge to share the gospel with Scott?

I once heard a pastor share a story about her faith journey. She explained how she had grown up a Christian, but as she became an adult and learned about other religions, she explored and experimented with many different ideas, values, and concepts until ending up back where she had begun. She found her way back to truth, the love of Christ and trusting in her Heavenly Father. I was with her and cheering inside until this next statement. She said she returned because it was comfortable, she felt welcome, and it was easy. My brain came to a screeching halt, and I had to hold on to my hand not to raise it in objection.

Don't get me wrong. We are always welcome and at home when we return to our Lord and Savior. Most churches and places of worship work diligently to ensure visitors or new believers feel accepted and comfortable so their hearts will be open to hearing the good news of the Gospel. But following Christ isn't always comfortable. It's hard, takes guts, and sometimes it hurts. It can be tough in these human and sinful bodies we walk around in, but it isn't supposed to be easy. In fact, it's in the uncomfortable that we grow the most. We grow stronger in our faith, stronger in our love for the Lord, and stronger in our trust of His laws and plan. Allen may not seem all that courageous in his act of simply handing Scott a CD or sharing his opinion about honesty, but in a world that screams and advertises "do what makes you happy," it can be challenging to remain faithful to God's values and step out to share your faith.

Count yourself blessed every time someone cuts you down or throws you out, every time someone smears or blackens your name to discredit me. What it means is that the truth is too close for comfort and that that person is uncomfortable. You can be glad when that happens—skip like a lamb if you like!— for even though they don't like it, I do... and all heaven applauds. And know that you are in good company; my preachers and witnesses have always been treated like this. Luke 6:22-23 (MSG)

As a Christian, sometimes it can feel as if our faith, love, and joy are being questioned and scrutinized from every angle. If you are a believer, have you ever felt like your prayers for others are seen as condescending, your joy as suspicious, your peace as naive and your generosity as frivolous? It takes guts and a load of faith to risk a friendship, job or relationship by staying true to God's ways and doing what's right. It takes fortitude and faith to step out and share your story of how God has worked in your life with someone you know isn't a believer. Scott may have never listened to the CD, but that didn't matter. Allen was following what God had called him to do. We don't have control of what others will do, but we can control our actions. Being obedient and allowing God to do the rest takes abundant faith.

Enter by the narrow gate. For the gate is wide and the way is easy that leads to destruction, and those who enter by it are many. For the gate is narrow and the way is hard that leads to life, and those who find it are few. Matthew 7:13-14 (ESV)

If you follow Christ, you have probably experienced and seen how it creates growing pains to enter through the narrow gate (Jesus). It's so effortless to tell our children to do whatever is right no matter how people treat them. "Stand up for the ones who can't stand up for themselves, even if you are teased. Don't be influenced by peer pressure and make poor decisions just to fit in," we teach them. "Just because everyone else is doing it doesn't make it right," we explain. But are we living that way for our children and those around us who are looking to us (as Christians) to set an example?

The wide gate, the gate of this world, is so easy to fit through, so simple to enter, it doesn't ruffle feathers or question anyone about their motives but leads to destruction. Destruction of so much more than we realize until it is too late because it is a slow erosion. Scott was being herded. Herded through the wide gate, trusting only the ones he followed behind, and not our Lord and Savior. It would have been effortless for Allen just to walk away from the business deal and make the decision not to do business with Scott again. To have left him lost in the crowd, but he didn't.

In Henry Cloud's book *How People Grow*[ii], he talks about having depression and how he was angry with God for not healing him through supernatural zapping until one day he realized that God's Plan A is people. As he looked back over his period of depression, he realized God had been placing specific people in his path—one with encouragement, one with a similar experience, one with hope, or one to listen. It was these people, he realized, that were God's plan to bring him out of depression. Not all at once, but in time. Plan A is usually the preferred plan. Do you think Allen was God's Plan A? Or do you think God had called someone to share the gospel with Scott years earlier, but they didn't follow through? You only move on to Plan B or Plan C if the desired plan doesn't work out. I'm sure God would have loved having Scott in His family earlier, but He never gives up on us. Scott, like each of us, is loved and adored by our Father in Heaven even when we turn our backs on Him. God will accomplish His plan with or without us, but He wants us in on it.

When I think back on all the opportunities I missed to be God's Plan A because my faith wasn't strong enough, my courage weak because it was my own and not His, my worth still tied up in past sins because I wasn't sure of His great love and forgiveness, my heart breaks. Now, I live daily to be His Plan A by staying in tune with His voice through prayer and reading scripture. By believing and trusting in His great plan even when all seems lost.

Is there something in the way of you following Jesus through the narrow gate today? Something in the way of you being used as His Plan A, following Him with your whole heart, and serving Him above all else?

Guilt, shame, resentment, distrust, sin, lack of faith, hate, fear, and anger (at God or someone else) can be considerable barriers to allowing God in so He can use for His glory. When we let these emotions get in the way, we are allowing Satan to win, and it's not just our hearts at stake but the hearts of God's other children that suffer.

As Christians, we are called to love others and share the good news with them. As Allen showed us, you don't even have to have the courage to say the words but to simply act, maybe just by giving someone a book or CD. Understanding that our courage and strength comes from God and not from ourselves helps. It's always such a relief to realize that He never created us to do these things without Him. Are you willing to sit face-to-face with someone, have the tough conversations, find comfort in the uncomfortable, stretch your faith, and seek the narrow gate?

We need to be ready for God to use us for His glory and plan, but also be careful about letting our pride, guilt, and disappointment cloud our judgment and actions. The problem occurs when we try to focus too much on what God is doing in us or through us, and not enough on God Himself. Allen has a remarkable story to tell others of how Scott came to the Lord through the simple act of giving him a CD, but what if Scott had never listened to it? What if Scott was still floundering in his faith? If Allen focused on the guilt and disappointment rather than the fact that he listened and responded to God's call, it could have been disastrous. Allen may have shut down and never shared his faith again. However, if we keep our eyes and hearts concentrated on what God has done for us, we will not fail. When we consider the great love He showed us by sacrificing His own Son on the cross so we could experience eternal forgiveness and life, we will not fail to follow the narrow gate, to keep our eyes on Him, His word as our foundation and receive His Godly wisdom. We are called to act according to His will, we demonstrate love and plant seeds; the rest is up to God.

James 3:17 tells us—*the wisdom that comes from heaven is first of all pure; then peace-loving, considerate, submissive, full of mercy and good fruit, impartial and sincere.*

Who doesn't want wisdom like that? On the other hand, if we choose the world over God, James 4:4 calls those adulterous people.

Adulteresses! Don't you know that friendship with the world is hostility toward God? So whoever wants to be the world's friend becomes God's enemy. James 4:4 (HCSB)

As disciples of Christ, we have a holy position. After reading these verses from Matthew 7 over and over again in my life, they convicted my heart in a new way. It was then that I began to strive and follow Christ with all my heart.

Knowing the correct password—saying 'Master, Master,' for instance— isn't going to get you anywhere with me. What is required is serious obedience—doing what my Father wills. I can see it now—at the Final Judgment thousands strutting up to me and saying, 'Master, we preached the Message, we bashed the demons, our God-sponsored projects had everyone talking.' And do you know what I am going to say? 'You missed the boat. All you did was use me to make yourselves important. You don't impress me one bit. You're out of here.'

These words I speak to you are not incidental additions to your life, homeowner improvements to your standard of living. They are foundational words, words to build a life on. If you work these words into your life, you are like a smart carpenter who built his house on solid rock. Rain poured down, the river flooded, a tornado hit—but nothing moved that house. It was fixed to the rock.

But if you just use my words in Bible studies and don't work them into your life, you are like a stupid carpenter who built his house on the sandy beach. When a storm rolled in and the waves came up, it collapsed like a house of cards. Matthew 7:21-27 (MSG)

Building on the rock involves strenuous work, guts, time and devotion in His word and staying in communication with our Heavenly Father. As Christians, we must strive, and labor to establish disciplines, surround ourselves with other believers, understand and follow Biblical truths, make Christ-centered choices and live above the world focused on the cross.

No, it isn't easy, but we don't have to die on the cross because Christ has already taken care of that. All we have to do is follow Him and be willing to step out in faith to share His good news and the story of how He has loved us. We are the only religion that has a risen Lord. That is the foundation of everything we believe. Let's stand up today and start living like we serve a Lord who is alive and reigning so no one can say, as Gandhi did, "I like your Christ! I do not like your Christians. Your Christians are so unlike your Christ."[iii]

Living this way and taking a chance like Allen did with Scott takes effort. It's not comfortable, and sometimes it hurts. God doesn't ring, whine, or pull at our shirts, but He does await you. He awaits your open and willing heart to receive His word and truth. His word changes us and makes us crave the uncomfortable, so we grow in our faith and gain life through Him.

PRAYER

Father, give us the courage and strength to keep our eyes on the cross, not the person in front of us. Not the numbers. Not the outcome, but on You. Living at the foot of the cross daily, seeking YOU above all else, making your word our foundation and praising you for it all. I pray you will direct and shape us so that going through the narrow gate feels more comfortable than the wide gate. That our hearts would beat only for You, and that our trust in You will guide our every thought, action, and deed. Give us eyes to see every opportunity to be and share your light and love. We adore you Father and are constantly in awe of your power and love for each of us despite our flaws. In Jesus's name, Amen.

ELLA

Planes hitting buildings on 9/11.
News of Osama Bin Laden's demise.
The space shuttle Challenger explosion.

Those heavy, impactful, life-altering moments are like indelible ink on our brains. We remember where we were and what we were doing when the news came. My list of moments like those includes when I heard that four-year-old Ella Newmiller had an inoperable tumor on her brain stem. Clear as day, I remember that I was sitting at lunch in a Chinese restaurant in North Raleigh with Allen (mentioned in Chapter 1).

The general rule with my wife, Jeanne, is that one phone call can be ignored if it needs to be, but multiple calls in succession tell you that something serious is up and the call should be answered. Allen and I were sitting at a table smack in the middle of the restaurant. This, coupled with the fact that I am not a phone guy when in public places, led me to listen more than I spoke when I took my wife's call. The words were sad, simple and direct, "Ella Newmiller has a brain tumor—that's why she's been out of preschool lately. The doctors say she has weeks to months." A few minutes later, another call came from my wife. She said, "Her fifth birthday is on Friday—her parents just want her to have a great birthday party."

The sadness in my wife's voice would have been enough. Later that day, Jeanne's description to me of her relationship with this little girl (who shared the same name as *our* daughter) sent me on a path that I can only describe as purposeful. After a few hours, Jeanne and I were at home together, and she shared the rest of the story. She told me that Ella's mother worked in the church where the two Ella's were in preschool together. Since she was there early each day, Ella would ask her mom if she could go downstairs to wait by the door—the door that, on a daily basis, magically produced a bunch of friends for her to play with at preschool. Just as the other parents did, Jeanne would walk our daughter Ella into the school. Each day, Jeanne would kiss our Ella goodbye. Apparently, after witnessing this a few times, Ella Newmiller would say, "Hey, where's *my* kiss?" There was no saying 'no' to that sweet face and sassy personality, so Jeanne had gotten into the habit of giving this little friend a smooch on the cheek. This story, told to me with tears in her eyes, put tears in mine and ignited a passion in me that remains to this day.

If the new-found passion was a key, the birthday party planning was the ignition. Within a matter of hours, "Team Ella" had been formed, and I was on it. The phone call at lunch with Allen had come on a Monday. Tuesday brought the first team meeting. By Wednesday we were in full-on, stay home from work, bust your behind, party planning mode. This little friend to my daughter and wife was now the main focus of my week and, is it turns out, future work.

For the most part, I believe that the different areas of our lives (personal, work, family, faith) are meant to be intermingled. When you allow the passions from your personal life to ooze into conversations in your work life, you show the world who you really are. Your authenticity in the eyes of others can skyrocket when they get the opportunity to see the whole you. In this case, the benefit of not "silo-ing" my life was made apparent—my huge network of contacts and friends I had made during my 15-year career helped tremendously as I remembered a contact for this and a contact for that to help make Ella's party awesome. Most of the phone calls were followed up by emails because my emotions wouldn't allow the words to flow as I reached out to people for favors, all in hopes of this sweet little girl getting the birthday party of all birthday parties.

She did.

Team Ella's planning and calling and emailing resulted in the best princess-themed party in the history of princess-themed parties. Ella and her family, dressed in royal clothing, arrived in a white, horse-drawn carriage. As they pulled up to the church, their arrival was announced by a tuxedo-clad gentleman as though they had just arrived at an 1800's gala in their honor. The smile on Ella's face at that moment and throughout the day made apparent that it was *our* honor to serve her and her family.

The fellowship hall on the second floor of Edenton Street United Methodist Church was overflowing with Ella's friends and teachers from the church preschool as well as many others who loved her. Throughout the day we all enjoyed a bubble machine, a DJ, visits from the mascots of local sports teams, a magician and cake (of course there was cake). Ella was deservedly provided a throne situated in a very prominent location, which she used as fatigue set in during the party.

A princess-themed birthday party of this weight and importance needs a REAL princess, I thought during those planning days that came before Friday's party. My attempt at the phone call to arrange a visit from a real princess was especially feeble as I could barely eek out the words to Beth, the Executive Director of the Miss North Carolina pageant. Fortunately, Beth blessed me with her email address and then quickly learned how she could help. And help she did. The crowning moment of the party was when Ella, in all her glory in a beautiful, sleeveless pink dress, was crowned by the reigning Miss North Carolina and two of her princess friends who had arrived in full pageant attire to love on Ella.

My two most memorable moments from that incredible day sit in framed photographs on my credenza. One from the very moment when the girls were crowning Ella and the other of Ella giving me a sweet kiss on my cheek as I held her in the courtyard of the church (after I bribed her, of course). She looked so tired at the end of that day, but I know her heart was full, as were the hearts of all who served her and her family at that unforgettable event.

*

"Weeks to months" is what the doctors had said upon her diagnosis. In her sassy fashion—the cornerstone of her lively personality—Ella wagged her finger at that prognosis and said, "Nut uh" as she proceeded to live for 1,381 days after her diagnosis. No one on Team Ella expected thanks for all the effort invested in the planning of her 5th birthday party, yet we *were* thanked with invitations to enjoy her 6th, 7th, and 8th as well. Our pink bracelets held these words, "Behold; I will do a new thing..." from Isaiah 43:19. He surely did a new thing by allowing us to have her for much longer than most of her counterparts who have shared the diagnosis of a DIPG brain tumor.

When Ella went to Heaven, she was at home with her family holding her in their arms. Ella's family did not want her journey through childhood cancer to conclude in a medical setting nor did they want her body preserved with chemicals after she passed. After being bathed and anointed with oils, her body was laid on her bed in her room, dressed in a beautiful, flowered cotton dress. I'll never forget the gasp I let out when a friend in the quiet-yet-busy house asked me if I wanted to go upstairs and see her when I went to pay my respects. I had driven 30 minutes to get to their home in Raleigh the day after she passed, yet for some reason, I had not prepared myself for that moment when I would be offered the chance to sit with her. Just as I remember that gasp, I remember the chill of the air from the open window in her room on that February day.

A simple pine casket had been made by a family friend. As Ella neared her new beginning, her mother had researched natural burials. This was an option not many knew about, yet we all stood fascinated by. The details included the omission of any chemicals, a cotton dress with no plastic or metal on it and a casket that had no screws or nails in it. Back to the earth via a natural burial seemed, well, natural.

It is hard to fathom how difficult it must have been to even *think about*—let alone *research*—options for the burial of your child, yet Ella's parents amazed us some more. In the living room of the Newmiller's modest home sat the casket; it sat there for the day and a half before her burial. During this time, friends were welcome to visit and, whether or not they went upstairs to see Ella, they were asked to decorate her casket with crayons and markers. Because of this unique and unexpected option for Ella's fans, the mood in the home was mixed when our family arrived on the morning of her funeral. There were plenty of tears among the din of children's voices as they played downstairs, on the back porch and in the yawning front yard. The words written on the casket that stuck with me—and apparently with the Priest as well (he mentioned them at her service)—were right next to, "I love you almost as much as chocolate toast." They said, "Have fun!" Apparently, one of her friends was wise beyond her years and knew that Ella was now going to be able to have fun in heaven, free from cancer and wheelchairs and doctors visits. Those words resonated so much with our family that they made their way onto bracelets we created and sold as a fundraiser and they also grace our backyard with brightly colored metal letters that sit beside our pool. "Have fun" is what that sweet little girl did; now we do the same in her memory.

At preschool, Ella Newmiller and five other girls including our Ella had earned themselves the nickname of "The Kissing Girls" for always trying to kiss the boys on the playground. I'll never forget the text I sent to the dad of one of the other Kissing Girls on the morning of the funeral—it said, "I can't believe what we're getting ready to do." We had been asked to don pink shirts, jeans, and boots in honor of Ella's favorite attire and be the pallbearers at her funeral.

Carrying a casket is an impressionable moment.

Carrying the casket of an eight-year-old girl is an unforgettable moment.

Physically handling the body of an eight-year-old girl from her room in her house downstairs to a casket specially made for her and decorated by her friends, then standing in the living room while her parents kiss her for the last time, say goodbye and place the cover over her is an impressionable, unforgettable, life-changing experience.

A natural burial was nothing I had ever heard of, nor had most who experienced Ella's goodbye. We gathered at the end of the driveway that had delivered us through the traditional cemetery. Where the pavement ended, a grassy path began. After Ella's perfectly decorated pine box that now held her body was placed in a vehicle, her family and all its supporters fell in behind it. As we walked down the tree-lined path that would lead us up to the wooded burial site, Ella's classmates from Our Lady of Lourdes Catholic School began to sing songs like "Amazing Grace." As if the setting wasn't serene enough, the beautiful lake that bordered one side of the path provided a gorgeous backdrop to it all. A look around during the graveside service in the woods that followed our procession revealed a couple of hundred sad faces of classmates, friends, parents, and family. Many of those sad faces turned to smiles as we shared stories and listened to Ella's recorded singing voice played through speakers that had been set up at the site. You could hear her young age in her voice as she sang "Jesus Loves Me" alongside her friend and worship leader, Stefan, who had recorded one of their many collaborations a few months before this day. The shock of hearing Ella's voice at such a moment as this one in the woods was greatly outweighed by the joy-filled memory we all had of Ella always wanting the microphone.

*

Ella's family will never be the same, nor will we who knew her and lived alongside her family during those difficult years, months, weeks and days. While we struggled, helpless to cure her, she taught us volumes about love, life, hope, and friendship. And for my family, in what could only be described as a "God thing," we learned of a place where Ella's spirit and light could shine on other families tackling similar challenges.

In July of 2012, five months after Ella's passing, our entire family was given the wonderful opportunity to love on and serve a family from Illinois at a retreat in Florida. The event was organized by Lighthouse Family Retreat, an organization that serves families living through childhood cancer by creating environments on seaside retreats where they can rest, restore relationships, experience joy and find hope in God. This retreat served twelve families from all over the country. Volunteers like The Wittig Family were there to serve and do all we could to take away the worries of life, if only for a week.

Just as the opportunity to serve a family in need affected me when planning Ella's party, the same kind of flutter and call from above happened about four minutes into our retreat. I found an opportune moment during "Flip Flop"—a time each morning when the Family Partners take all the kids to the pool or beach for a couple of hours of fun in the sun. This time allows the parents of the child in treatment time to gather at a meeting appropriately called "Common Grounds" where they share their stories and their tears. I approached the Executive Director and expressed my interest in helping to grow Lighthouse out of Florida and into our state of North Carolina. As the conversation progressed from that day at our first retreat in Florida, this verse became my guide, "I'm doing a great work; I can't come down. Why should the work come to a standstill so that I can come down to see you?" (Nehemiah 6: 2-3, MSG) Those words resonated because squeezing another "thing" into an already busy life with small children and work was going to prove challenging. However, nothing was going to cause me to stop this work, and no work or job or person was going to stop this thing.

Nothing would be allowed to interfere with my efforts, which included learning all I could about how non-profits functioned, raising money and spreading the word about this wonderful ministry through speeches and emails and conversations. To be clear, I had no assurance whatsoever that the organization would want or need to start a local chapter to run retreats in our state, let alone that they would want me to be involved; they weren't even fully decided on expansion. All I needed was the passion for serving families like Ella's that was born at her 5th birthday party to become coupled with these words from the Executive Director at poolside that day, "Funny you should ask about us expanding—I just got hired for this position recently, and I told the board that I would like to look to expand retreats outside of Florida." Tell me my chances are one in a million and I'll be just like Jim Carrey in *Dumb and Dumber*, "So you're tellin' me there's a chance!"

I treated the next two years as the world's longest job interview. I drove to Atlanta twice for meetings I didn't have to go to, I took classes toward a certificate in non-profit management at Duke University, I networked, I raised over $20,000, I sought out locations for North Carolina retreats, I met with doctors and nurses who could refer families for us to serve, I gave speeches, I helped at another retreat, I got my family to agree to downsize our house so we could afford it if I worked for a non-profit and made less money, I got back with the Miss North Carolina pageant and gained the support of the entire pageant, I, I, I...

In the end, I realized it wasn't about "I"—it was about the families. The job didn't happen, and I've since gotten clarity that my role was simply to do all I could to help get a retreat started in my home state, just like I asked about poolside at our family's first retreat. Doing so would serve more families like Ella's.

The first retreat to ever be held outside of Florida happened in 2014 and was, indeed, held in North Carolina. What I realized after it happened was that this whole thing was a big ole faith test. It *was* about me, yet not in terms of "*me* this and *me* that" outlined above, but in the sense that I had been given an opportunity to serve a family through a very difficult time to be given another opportunity to serve *multiple* families through a very difficult time. I did all of this with absolute faith that it was the right thing for me to do at that time in my life. This wasn't about Scott starting a chapter of Lighthouse Family Retreat in North Carolina but rather how God can use Scott and his contacts and personality and passion to serve a ministry that serves hundreds.

Mess to message: *A birthday party and an incredibly sad, memorable, life-changing day in the woods connects with an organization that we will always be connected to. A passion was ignited, and it continues to fire in service to families who can benefit from it. Thank you, Ella, for letting me be a part of your journey and for showing me the way toward greater service to others.*

Another good that came from this whole experience was the opportunity to work with my Ella on a children's book. Entitled, "Two Ella's," it tells the story about that special day at Ella Newmiller's birthday party. Email Scott at scottwittig.com and I will send you a copy.

† PRISONERS OF HOPE †

What if Scott had been on the other side of the world, just as many of the Newmiller's prayer warriors were, and wasn't able to step in and help plan the party or attend the funeral? What happens when life is altered in such a way that you see one of your worst nightmares play out around you? What's left to do when actions and words can't heal or help?

I knew Ella too. My daughter was one of the "Kissing Girls" that Scott mentioned. I had the incredible blessing and privilege to be there with a small tribe of women to help prepare Ella's body for burial. I still remember the feeling of washing her face with a warm washcloth and anointing her with oil. There aren't words that can describe what that moment meant and the emotions that are stored away in my heart, but I can tell you it was a sacred experience and I, like so many, will never be the same. We tell our children about the cycle of life. We explain that you are born, you live, grow old, and then you die. What happens when that idea is turned upside down?

Scott listened, loved and went into action. He was present and able to be the hands and feet of Christ with a multitude of others who loved Ella and her family. But what if you aren't able to be the hands and feet of Christ? What's left? What if you are battling cancer yourself, are on the other side of the country and can't deliver a meal or just don't have the resources of time or money to give?

There is a simple, but powerful answer - prayer. With prayer, you can be God's heart. You can love and pray from anywhere, and it doesn't take many resources but just a little time. I can tell you from knowing and being around this family that, from the moment Ella was diagnosed until the time she joined her Heavenly Father, hope and prayer were front and center.

So often, when we face great sadness, overwhelming obstacles and horrific circumstances our hands and feet begin moving in reaction. It is human nature to try and make the situation better in some way. In any way that we can. However, when we do that, we take one of the most formidable weapons we have available to defeat despair, grief, disease, and agony and toss it aside. I'm a spring into action, Type A girl, so I have to fight the lie that prayer isn't enough because PRAYER IS ENOUGH and sometimes it's all we have. However, it should always be our first defense. We should seek God first, not just for answered prayers but for wisdom, direction, strength, and courage to face the mountain before us.

Ella had an army of prayer warriors around the world. Many of them knew her and just as many didn't. It was an incredible time to witness the power and love of Christ at work in His church. Ella's mom told me time and time again how she felt those prayers. She understood how the strength, courage, wisdom, comfort, and peace she needed as she watched her child suffer was not of her own. Although God didn't answer the #1 prayer of complete healing this side of Heaven for Ella, He made Himself known to them, and her parent's faith remained strong. It reminds me so much of Shadrach, Meshach, and Abednego from the book of Daniel.

King Nebuchadnezzar had entrusted three Jewish men, who were far from home and essentially prisoners in a foreign land, with many responsibilities and elevated them within his ranks. Everything was going fine until the King decided to build a big gold idol of himself for everyone to bow down and worship. Although, when Shadrach, Meshach, and Abednego were given the ultimatum to fall down and worship the king and his gods or be burned in the fiery furnace, they chose the furnace! Not only that, they said:

If the God we serve exists, then He can rescue us from the furnace of blazing fire, and He can rescue us from the power of you, the king. But even if He does not rescue us, we want you as king to know that we will not serve your gods or worship the gold statue you set up. Daniel 3:17-18 (HCSB)

They realized and trusted that God could save them if He chose to, but "even if He didn't" they would not give in and turn away from Him. Sometimes we forget that God created the world with evil as part of the original fabric of life. In fact, in Genesis, as He looked out upon all He had created, he thought it was awesome (Genesis 1:31). It's after mankind and the free will God granted us hit the scene that evil enters the picture.

How many people do you know who haven't gotten what they wanted from God and have turned from Him out of anger, resentment or disgust? I have met quite a few, and it breaks my heart to see what they are missing out on just because they didn't get what they desired or thought they deserved. Like Shadrach, Meshach, and Abednego, Ella's parents realized something that we may tend to forget at times; *Our God is the...God who holds your life-breath in His hand and who controls the whole course of your life.* (excerpt of Daniel 5:23)

When we allow that to sink into our hearts, we can experience radical change and learn to trust God more boldly than we ever imagined. I pray as we trust and look to God for direction through prayer, He will honor us with clear answers, blessings, and revelations, but EVEN IF HE DOESN'T, we will praise Him. (Daniel 2:20-23)

Instead of being prisoners of fear, prisoners of doubt, or prisoners of despair may we all be prisoners of hope and bold with our prayers. (Zechariah 9:12)

The definition of a prisoner is a person who feels confined or trapped by circumstances or a certain situation. I can't think of anything I would rather be held captive to more than hope. As Christians, our faith in the Lord our God comes from the confidence we have in knowing, believing, and trusting in Him above all else.

In the book of Zechariah, we see hope-filled prisoners receive some fantastic news.

Rejoice greatly, Daughter Zion! Shout, Daughter Jerusalem! See, your king comes to you, righteous and victorious. lowly and riding on a donkey, on a colt, the foal of a donkey. Zechariah 9:9 NIV

Step out of yourself for a moment and sit in the crowd with them as they listen to future promises. Imagine all of the trials, anguish, pain, and disruption their families had endured. Now they were standing there listening to Zechariah share a message from God; not just any message, but a spectacular message that included the promise of a coming King that would save them and restore their nation. Not only will He appear and bring restoration, but His arrow will flash like lightning, His trumpet will sound, He will shield them, save them, and overcome their enemies with only a slingshot because that is our God! (Zechariah 9:14-17) He is awesome! He is able! He is mighty! He is just! He is truth! He is light! He is faithful! He is merciful! He is our KING! This good news is for all of us.

Ella understood hope. Even at the age of eight, she believed and trusted that Jesus had come, died, and paid for our sins ensuring we would have eternal life. Where pain and sadness exist, there can also be prayer, faith, and joy.

- Faith in a God who has a perfect plan even when it seems like a mess to us,
- Joy and comfort in understanding the eternal life we have access to as believers in Christ, and
- Prayer to stay connected to the source of all faith, joy, hope, and love because we can't survive and sustain ourselves without the True Source of Life, our Heavenly Father.

Are you a prisoner of hope or a prisoner of doubt?

On those days when you aren't sure what to pray, are overcome with grief, busyness or such undesirable circumstances you can't think straight, but know you need to be on your knees in prayer with God, Psalm 86 is for you. It is called David's Prayer. It is a treasure and covers all we need from the Lord daily. I call it my "God Please" prayer.

PRAYER (from Psalm 86)
Heavenly Father, please answer me (v. 1), protect my life (v. 2), be gracious to me (v. 3), bring joy to my life (v.4), make me rich in faithful love (v. 5), listen to my pleas (v. 6) and answer me (v. 7), teach me your ways and give me an undivided mind to fear to your name (v. 11), turn to me and be gracious to me, give me Your strength (v. 16), show me a sign of your goodness, help and comfort me (v. 17). In Your Son's Mighty name, Amen.

MARK & TODD

Mark is Ella's dad. Todd is Ellie's dad.

I say 'is' because *they* say 'is.' There are no rules about what you're allowed to say or what words to use when you've gone through what these guys have gone through. They will always be their daughters' dad; it's just that now their daughters are guiding their actions instead of the other way around—the way it was when they were physically present in their dad's lives.

Before greeting him at his car in the church parking garage and ushering his family to the carriage that awaited them for Ella's party, I wouldn't have known Mark if I knocked him over on the street. We shared the title of, "Father of a *Kissing Girl*" but hadn't shared any conversation until that day. Today, I'm proud to call him a friend; a friend who has returned the favor of kindness in many ways since the day of that memorable fifth birthday party.

I had knocked on Todd's front door once or twice to drop Ella off for sleepovers and play dates with his middle daughter Grace who, along with her younger sister Anna, attended the same school as our children; the school where my wife teaches and had Ellie in class just before she passed. After knocking ever-so-gently on that same front door at 7 a.m. to hand him a bag of bagels and gallon of coffee two days after his 14 year-old-daughter, Ellie had succumbed to a brain aneurysm; I chatted with Todd for a few minutes. Before my feet touched the sidewalk after stepping off his front porch, I knew I would one day call him a friend just as I do with Mark.

Special Guys With Special Daughters—that is the title they hold with me.

When you are in your late thirties and early forties, and you have children, your life is kid-focused, no doubt. Mark and Todd were no different and, therefore, at the same place in life as I was. It was because of this that I paid very close attention to their incredible poise and strong faith as they supported their wives and families through inarguably the toughest of tough times a father could ever experience. Ella's journey from diagnosis to Heaven lasted years while Ellie's lasted hours, yet the process of accepting friends and saying goodbye was neither too different for Mark and Todd. With each handshake and hug came rattling loose a memory from their daughter's short-time on this earth. I watched them handle the receiving lines with grace, both of them leaning on their character and sense of humor to get them through what has got to be so, so painful. Mark said, "It wasn't a conscious decision to be strong." "It's what dad's do," Todd told me.

Since the sadness of those receiving lines, both of these men have experienced happiness, and they have done so with those same people they welcomed at their daughter's goodbyes. You see, the good that has come from the devastation they have experienced has been very similar for Mark and Todd. I learned this when I had the opportunity to introduce the two of them over coffee. As I was driving to meet them that morning, I had a thought that was not dissimilar to the one I had the morning of Ella's funeral, *"I can't believe what I'm getting ready to do."* Facilitating a discussion with two grieving fathers about their experience with loss is not something I would ever say I *wanted* to do, but I am forever grateful that I did it because of the lessons learned from the loss.

*

How fast your perspective can be changed. The over-arching theme of this book is that good can come from not-so-good. It's not literary prose that keeps me from saying 'bad' but my belief that the life experiences written about in these pages are of value and goodness in some way. The experiences may suck. They may be immensely painful to get through. They may seem horribly unfair. They may be all of the above, but they also serve a purpose. Mark's perspective on those words was enlightening, yet his attention went not to the lack of 'bad' but the presence of 'good' in the words I am using as a filter throughout this book. "I don't think 'good' is the right word to use to describe this," Mark said. "You can use it in the book, Scott, but I prefer to say the 'change' or 'positive things' that came from losing Ella. Her death wasn't 'good,' but I can say that there are some positive things that came out of it."

I may have to take back what I said six paragraphs earlier, the part about there not being rules about what words to use when you've gone through what these guys have gone through. While Todd seemed to agree with Mark, neither got up and left the table. For that, I thank God because the concoction of vulnerability and kindness within these men produced such a valuable discussion about changes in their behavior, in their families and those around them.

In their behavior
"I've changed how I interact with other people. I tell my friends how I feel a lot more than I used to." -Mark

In their families
"My family is closer now. We try to understand each other more." -Todd

In those around them
Todd said his non-Christian co-workers saw his steadfast faith and wondered what they were missing (missing out on).

Mark said many conversations about faith resulted among his ninth-grade son's friends that may not have happened otherwise.

"Some co-workers noticed there were a few people avoiding me because they didn't know what to say. My company ended up holding a 'grief in the workplace' webinar that has helped all of us in so many ways." –Todd

When they spoke about the support they got from everyone around them, Mark and Todd agreed that it brought a light into the darkness that they needed so very much. They felt as though they saw the face of God by way of all the love that was poured into them. Todd said he was thankful when people would do *something*, even if solely through prayer while Mark said he was thankful to have the perspective that said, "Who am I to stop people from helping?"

*

'Family Bingo Night' at Thales Academy (the school Todd's daughter had attended) was put together to benefit the Brain Aneurysm Foundation in memory of Ellie. While sitting in one of the classrooms waiting for the games to begin I saw Todd standing in the hallway by himself, so I got up to say hello. After shaking his hand, I told him I was about to write a chapter about the good that can come from the not-so-good of losing a child. Before he could say anything, I put my arms out to the sides with palms up and motioned toward all of the people filling the classrooms around us. We both smiled. Family's spending quality time together. Kids hanging out with teachers with no chance of homework being assigned. A family getting to watch love in action in support of a cause they never knew would be *their* cause. Todd said, "The NBA used to have the slogan 'Where Amazing Happens.' We've seen that time after time since Ellie died, just like we have tonight. It's so awesome."

Amazing has happened for both families through…
- "Ella's Race"—an annual fundraiser that brings together hundreds of people and thousands of dollars to support pediatric brain tumor research. (www.ellasrace.com)

- Entire student bodies wearing pink or ball caps to bring attention to the cause.
- Scholarships being created.
- Lobbyists are paying attention and channeling efforts toward funding for research and awareness of brain aneurysms.

One of the most poignant moments of our 65-minute conversation over coffee came when Todd told of two defining moments in his life that came before—and perhaps **prepared him for**—the tumult of losing a child. Todd shared that he had almost died two years before Ellie died, in a car wreck that kept him out of work for four months. He also told of friends who lost a child at birth. "The accident got us ready—our faith circle (support system) had already formed," Todd said. "Our friends never got a second with their child—we got 14 years with ours." Less than a year removed from burying his daughter, Todd had the perspective that many of us could go a lifetime without learning.

We are all put here to help each other; that is what these men believe. I guess it comes as no surprise that both are in careers that provide service to others…or that Mark and his wife have since completed the adoption of two young siblings from Haiti, fulfilling on a family plan that was hatched before Ella was diagnosed…or that Todd and his family have been successful with getting "Ellie's Law" (H.R. 594) introduced in Congress, a law that will authorize $25 million in federal funding for brain aneurysm research.

As years have passed, I have watched these families go from paralyzing devastation to functioning at a level just enough to get by and all the way up to the altruistic acts described above. While in the throws of something so horrible, it is easy to get lost in the notion that the dark clouds will never part; this I know from the conversations with these men. Witnessing first hand how light has replaced that darkness provides a testament that *it is possible*. The loss of a child is considered by many to be the worst experience any parent could ever experience and, while Ella and Ellie are thought of every day by their dads and their families, these parents have found ways to honor those memories in ways that will have a ripple effect for years and years to come.

Mess to message: *Thank you, Mark and Todd, for demonstrating for men how to lead your family through a tragedy and how to embrace all the change and the good and the positive things produced from the spirit of a child lost.*

† THE MOUNTAIN BEFORE ME †

What if Mark and Todd didn't have a deep and abiding faith? How would their message have been altered? There is so much pain and sadness in the world today, will it ever end? How do you stand to face your greatest nightmare living out before you?

I don't care how strong your faith may be; sometimes there are things that will never make sense this side of Heaven. I often wonder if God chose the redemption of man through the death of His son because He knew that losing a child would be one of the greatest pains His people would ever have to overcome. This way, those who had to endure such a tremendous loss would know they are not alone and serve a God who understands their deep pain.

There was once a great and prosperous city that fell to its enemies. It was destroyed, plundered and its people were taken prisoner to a foreign land. The book of Lamentations says this about that great city.

How deserted lies the city,
once so full of people!
How like a widow is she,
who once was great among the nations!
She who was queen among the provinces
has now become a slave.
Bitterly she weeps at night,

tears are on her cheeks.
Among all her lovers
there is no one to comfort her.
All her friends have betrayed her;
they have become her enemies.
After affliction and harsh labor,
Judah has gone into exile.
She dwells among the nations;
she finds no resting place.
All who pursue her have overtaken her
in the midst of her distress.
The roads to Zion mourn,
for no one comes to her appointed festivals.
All her gateways are desolate,
her priests groan,
her young women grieve,
and she is in bitter anguish. Lamentation 1:1-4 (NIV)

The words in these passages that stand out to me are: deserted, widow, slave, betrayal, affliction, harsh, overtaken, desolate, grief, and no resting place.

These verses describe a city, but surely Mark and Todd can relate. In fact, there are many who, like this city, are facing a deep and profound loss or destruction. They may be unsure of what their next step will be, fearful of where they will go, and feel as if they captives in a strange new land that doesn't make sense. How can a parent know what will life will look like after the loss of a child? How could a parent not be fearful of the overwhelming grief, questioning, and emptiness in their heart and home? Do they feel like prisoners in a strange land they want desperately to escape and wish everything could be as it once was?

Where did they, and where do we, find the faith to see past the moment, the grief, and despair? To trust and have the courage to face what's lies ahead?

I look up to the mountains;
does my strength come from mountains?
No, my strength comes from GOD,
who made heaven, and earth, and mountains.
    He won't let you stumble,
your Guardian God won't fall asleep.
Not on your life! Israel's
Guardian will never doze or sleep.
    GOD's your Guardian,
right at your side to protect you—
Shielding you from sunstroke,
sheltering you from moonstroke.
    GOD guards you from every evil,
he guards your very life.
He guards you when you leave and when you return,
he guards you now, he guards you always. Psalm 121 (MSG)

When most people go to the beach; they collect many shells. When I go to the beach, I collect a shell — just one. I don't want a collection, but a distinct memory from my trip. As I walk along the beach talking with my Lord and Savior, one usually catches my eye, and the Lord nudges me to scoop it up and treasure it. Several years ago, I enjoyed a quiet walk on the beach, and a beautiful shell caught my eye. Just as I reached down to pick it up, a rogue wave came blowing up. There was no doubt in my mind the shell had washed away. However, as the wave hurried back into the ocean, the shell remained. I gently picked it up and turned it over inspecting it from side to side and front to back.

"Why this shell, God?" I quietly thought to myself. It wasn't perfect or complete, but just the remains of a shell; the twists, turns and soft edges had given way to the wear and tear it had endured as it made the arduous journey from being a creature's home to vacancy, and eventually the shore. It was beautiful to me. I held it in my hand and continued my walk. It was interesting how my grip perfectly fit the twist and turns of the shell almost as if someone was grasping my hand. But in the back of my mind, I wondered if this imperfect shell was the right one to take home — my one shell.

A few minutes later, my eye caught another shell. This one was completely different. It was perfect and shiny like a small piece of polished glass, so beautiful that I couldn't resist inspecting it more closely. Again, as I stooped down to pick it up, a wave rolled in, but this time the shell was gone when the tide had receded. No longer an option for me to consider.

And that is when God whispered the answer of this mystery to my heart. "Allison, the second shell represents the shiny and temporary things of this world that vie for your attention. They seem perfect and beautiful but melt away after temporarily satisfying you. Their job is to draw you away from Me and slowly siphon your faith, hope, and joy until you are only an empty shell. But the first shell represents your life. This journey, although difficult at times, is a gift."

God can be so tender with His lessons and reminders. The shell was a tangible reminder to me that life will always take twists and turns. Waves will crash over our beliefs and may even seem to overtake us for a time. There will be many things we'll have to endure, but God will use them to make us beautiful in our own way. God doesn't like evil, but He does take it all, the good and the bad, to mold us and shape us into something beautiful. Each one of us is unique with our own story and scars. Just as Mark and Todd do, each one of us has a unique story with unique scars that we can share for the glory of God if we choose to.

I want to leave you with these words, the promises to those prisoners spoken of in Lamentations from the prophet Zechariah. I pray these words will challenge, convict and encourage you to push aside anything that may hinder you growing in faith, courage, and joy. That way, when the day comes that you face a storm of your own, you will know exactly who to turn to.

Once again men and women of ripe old age will sit in the streets of Jerusalem, each of them with cane in hand because of their age. The city streets will be filled with boys and girls playing there.

I will save my people from the countries of the east and the west.

The seed will grow well, the vine will yield its fruit, the ground will produce its crops, and the heavens will drop their dew. Zechariah 8:1-7, (NIV)

Playing, saved, grow, yield, and produce are the words I hear now. God's ways are not our ways, and we may not understand now, but His promises of protection and provision have never failed and will not fail now. The end of the story has already been written. Satan has lost, and we can trust that God will return, all suffering will end, and He will judge all evil.

PRAYER
God, you are more than just a name. You set the planet in motion and threw the stars in the sky. The mountains bow down to your great majesty. As we face heartache that seems too much to overcome, I pray we remember that you can do immeasurably more than we can even think of asking you. Please give us a holy courage to lean into You and rely on you when all seems lost so that you can turn our despair into restoration and our hope a reality. In Your Son Jesus's name, Amen.

DALE & LILA

On a Saturday morning in April, two months after Ella Newmiller's passing, Jeanne and I sat in our living room chatting with our company for the weekend—my best friend from college, Steve (here forth called 'Pelle' for his last name, Pellegrino) and the beautiful person he somehow got to marry him, Heather. My coffee hadn't had time to jolt me awake quite yet; its task was replaced by my mother's tone of voice in an uncharacteristically early phone call from her room at the nursing home.

"Your dad is sick. He just called me and told me it took him three hours to make his dinner last night. He kept passing out and coming back into consciousness, I guess. He's been feeling bad since Wednesday but didn't tell anyone."

At that point, my father had been fighting diabetes for 50 years. While the disease had robbed him of his ability to take care of my mother and her stroke-ravaged body, it had yet to take away his ability to live in an apartment on his own or drive himself to spend time with his wife. His visits to see my mom were as regular as his blood sugar spikes and drops, yet he had fallen off-schedule that week because he wasn't feeling well. He wasn't feeling well because he had contracted a nasty staph infection that was quickly taking its toll on his lungs and kidneys; this is what my visiting friend, Pelle, and I learned over the course of that Saturday we spent with my father in the emergency room. We sat with him and did what we could to soothe him and keep his mind off things, yet he did a pretty good job of handling that himself by telling jokes to the doctors and nurses. He had his sense of humor intact, but it was hard to hear the punchlines through his oxygen mask.

Dinnertime came and, while there wasn't food offered to him, a room upstairs in the hospital had been. "He'll be going to the Critical Care Unit, and the nurses will need to work with him alone for at least a couple of hours," is what we were told. "You should go ahead and go to the concert. Have fun. We'll take care of your dad."

It wasn't the opportunity to see my smiling face and shiny head that had brought Pelle into town—he had driven in to see Van Halen in concert with me and another college friend. We had a 45-minute highway drive to get there and figured we would take the nurse's advice and go have fun. Doing two 360's at 70mph in the rain on the highway in the dark may be construed as "fun" by some until their car hits a guardrail and quickly becomes scrap metal.

We heard the Van Halen show was awesome.

The next morning, after countless apologies to Heather and Pelle for their horrific visit that was filled with a day-long emergency room sojourn and an evening that involved emergency vehicles, we said goodbye. Neither of us had been injured, but Pelle and I were both shaken—the length of our man hug-handshake proved it.

After our guests headed home to South Carolina, my wife took me to my father's apartment. I needed a car to drive, and his Honda hybrid was of no use to him in a hospital bed. I'd much rather have had to rent a car than have his so readily available, but it was a blessing nonetheless.

*

Had my mother been able to walk, she could have gotten her release from the nursing home and walked about 300 yards across the hospital campus to visit my dad. Instead, I enlisted the help of the social work staff to arrange for wheelchair transport to get her there. After spending some time in Room 3 of the CCU, Mom and I went down to the cafeteria for something to eat. As we were making our way down one of the long, window-lined hallways on the second floor of the hospital, the Hospitalist in charge of my father's care stopped us to talk. He first stated the obvious—that my dad's defense system had been significantly weakened by his 50-year diabetes fight. The next words hit hard, "This infection could get him." After delivering words like that to the relatives of patients, I guess that doctors are very used to hearing what I said next, "You know *you* get to tell him that, Doc, because I can't."

After the doctor obliged and shared that tough reality with my dad, the conversation that needed to happen happened. What was interesting is that my father's eyes told me
...he already knew.
...he was tired.
...he felt horrible.

This fight he was fighting was not just a day or two old; it had been fought with syringes and insulin for years. After the doctor left, I grabbed hold of all the fortitude I could and, with my mother still in the room I said, "So, Dad, if the worst happens and this infection gets you, I know you want to be cremated but where do you want to be buried?" I will never—not until my last breath—forget what he said next. "Ella. Where Ella was buried, I want that. The natural burial."

My father had changed his wishes after hearing the story of that beautiful, yet so very sad, day that we said goodbye to little Ella Newmiller. Five days later we granted that last wish when we buried my father about five plots from where we had buried Ella—in that same wooded burial ground—not two months earlier. That little girl, who fought so hard for 1,381 days, had shown my father to his final resting place after his days of fighting had ended.

*

A friend of mine who is a public speaker recently posted, "The beginning of a most difficult day has begun. How do you say goodbye to your father who has been there for you your entire life?" My reply was, "You do what you do so well—you prepare and give a speech that is educational, candid, emotional and humorous...and you call it a eulogy." I had this perspective to share with him not only because that's exactly what I did when I gave my father's eulogy but my mother's as well, which I found myself delivering less than two years after my father passed.

Three losses in two years. All three of those loved ones buried in the same place. I learned a lot about natural burials and funerals in the woods. I also learned a lot about loss.

After Heaven gained Ella, the passion and energy that flowed from me and into Lighthouse Family Retreat's mission were welcomed. It was so cathartic to have a positive place to put that grief. How to do the same after losing both of my parents within two years of each other? The good to come from these extremely not-so-good experiences came flowing out when I wrote and delivered their eulogies.

Of my father, I said,

"Have you ever used humor to brighten someone's day because you could tell they could use it?

Have you ever given a complete stranger a hug because you saw they were upset?

Have you ever helped an old lady with her groceries?

I did all of those things...THIS WEEK...because of my dad. He did those things all the time, and I'm thankful he passed those gifts on to me.

The last thing I said to him on Monday night, while he was still with us, was "I love you." The last thing I said to him on Tuesday morning, after he was gone, was "Thank you for being my dad."

We are all better for knowing my dad."

Of my mother, I said,

"As you may have read in her obituary, she also greatly supported my sister through her challenges with bipolar disorder & a severe learning disability, and my mom took care of my dad who lived with diabetes for 50yrs. I'm a firm believer in finding the good in the not-so-good—the blessings that came from these two huge challenges in her life are:

1) A daughter who is thriving by sharing her gift of music by teaching flute and piano lessons for a living and,
2) We had an incredibly healthy and well-nourished family because my mom insisted on balanced meals and a strict mealtime schedule in support of my dad."

The gifts of loss can be many. While it is far easier to be sad, mad and bitter, it is far more rewarding and renewing to take the great traits and lessons learned from those lost and do something good with them.

You read about the humor, the hug and the help I credited my father with in his eulogy and my mother's kindness to my sister and father in hers; those things were identified *in reflection*. After those losses, though, I proceeded to find myself doing things with my parent's memory and their positive influence as a filter for *the present*. The situations described below occurred shortly after one or both of my parents had passed. As they were presented to me, my mind immediately went into "What-would-Mom-and-Dad-do?" mode:

A friend couldn't make it to a father-son outing for our YMCA group—I offered to take his son along with my son and me so he could still have that experience. We had a blast.

While running an errand on a Sunday morning, I saw a family in their Sunday-best standing outside their disabled car—I packed the four adults and one child in my two-door car and got them to the church on time.

The day after we moved into a new, smaller home, we were asked to keep a friend of our son's for a week so the parents could go away to handle a private situation—we took him in, and the parents handled whatever it was that they needed to handle.

Mess to message: *Thank you, Mom and Dad. I would like to say that these are all actions I would have taken and said 'yes' to before your passing, but I can't. Having acknowledged your kindness aloud in the woods on those two Fridays in April (two years apart) has allowed me to have the good of you as a filter that has allowed me to easily say 'yes' and proceed to do right by others.*

† WHERE DO YOU DWELL? †

I know a lot of positive change occurred from the lessons Scott learned, but what did he do with the loneliness he felt after losing his parents? Where does that fit in? What if Scott had crawled into a pit of anger and sadness after losing both his parents? What if his responses had been to allow his faith to grow stagnant instead of blossom and thrive?

A friend of mine once asked me to pray for her. She expressed how she was in a "dry" place. She had faced many challenges and obstacles over the past months, and it had taken a toll on her spirit. Even though she couldn't identify a specific prayer request, she knew she needed a lift. Her request made me think back on times in my own life when I felt like I was in the desert or a dry place with the Lord.

Webster's Online Dictionary defines desert as 1) Arid land with usually sparse vegetation; an area of water devoid of life 2) A wild, uninhabited and uncultivated tract 3) A desolate or forbidding area.

That definition certainly doesn't make you want to book an airline ticket to head off to the desert for your next vacation. Even when you are a Christian, the "desert times" can be stressful and scary, make us question our relationship with God and question God Himself. At the time, if given a choice, Scott may have chosen to skip this part of his life or fast-forward through it.

As Scott illustrated, life often requires a change in perspective. So, what if we look at the desert in a different light and give it a new definition? If you search for scriptures throughout the book of Exodus you notice that God called His people to worship me in the desert (Exodus 7:16), journey into the desert to offer sacrifices to the Lord our God (Exodus 3:18), hold a festival to me in the desert (Exodus 5:1). They looked toward the desert, and there was the glory of the LORD appearing in the cloud (Exodus 16:10).

In scripture, we see that the desert can be a good place, but it is up to us to meet God there with an open mind and a trusting heart. If God is there with us and we believe that He is who is says He is, we can praise Him in that desert place.

On the flip side of that, the desert can be all that Webster's describes if we lose sight of God and start to grumble as the Israelites did on their well-known journey through the desert. A trip through the desert *with* God can provide festival, praise, growth, and worship just as a trip through the desert *without* Him can bring thirst, defeat, and death.

God usually speaks to us through prayer, the Bible, those we encounter and our circumstances. Let's focus on the last one. Our circumstances can bring us to that desert place, and if we open our heart to the Lord, He can fill it with answers and speak to us in ways we wouldn't hear or understand if we were not in the desert. Scott told us himself that he may have never facilitated those random acts of kindness before the death of his parents. He learned as many have, that fruit can grow in abundance after a great pruning.

During the "dry times" we can learn to:
- Seek God daily for courage, direction, and peace through prayer and His written Word. Yes, it takes practice, devotion, prayer, study and a "No But's" kind of attitude.

- Ask God questions and get to know Him more intimately by reading about His character and qualities in scripture. We discover balance, change, peace, humility, confidence and so much more when we seek to know Him personally.
- Remember not to take God for granted when times are good because, in the dry times, we build discipline and a thirst to seek Him that we can carry with us during all our days.
- Reach out to God in our daily lives, no matter what good or bad is swirling around us because when we do, we find He is always there and cares enough to shelter and carry us through it all.
- Count on God. He will not leave you for forsake you.

Let's redefine the desert.

Desert: 1) Vast land that grows the bread of life; an area filled with the living water 2) A wild and exciting place full of opportunities to gain knowledge and grow closer with our Father in Heaven 3) An intimate and pleasant area

Now that's better!!!

He split rocks in the wilderness and gave them drink abundantly as from the deep. Psalm 78:15 (ESV)

Then he led out his people like sheep and guided them in the wilderness like a flock. Psalm 78:52 (ESV)

To him who led his people through the desert, His love endures forever. Psalm 136:16 (ESV)

But what happens when you are waiting in the desert and praying for a new perspective? What do we do in the wait? And what do we do if after all that praying the answer we wanted never comes? After all, we are human and to get from heartache to joy there are usually some emotions we have to wrestle with on the journey.

I've wrestled with God. Thank goodness, He has always won, but it can be ugly. I'm usually the "Let's look at the bright side of things" girl, maybe out of survival for all the things I've experienced and endured, or perhaps I was just born that way. However, there are still times when I feel like sitting down and screaming at all the evil around me or become so overwhelmed with all the pain and prayer requests I just need to sit and cry.

Singing songs to a troubled heart is like taking off clothing on a cold day or like pouring vinegar on soda. Proverbs 25:20 (HCSB)

Sometimes, people don't need an answer, a solution or a "Don't worry, be happy" song. They need someone to cry with. Solomon wisely explains that to a weeping person, stories of unicorns and daisies can be damaging and make things worse than they already are. I know I don't always enjoy it when someone tries to bring sunshine to my rainy day. There are times I need a short pity party.

We frequently hear, "Stay or get out of the pit" because it's a dangerous place to go. Not surprisingly, I have a different angle on the pit. I'm all for it as long as there are guidelines. I think we all reach a place in life, now and then, where we can benefit from getting into the pit and rolling around in our grief or misery. However, you can only go if you know you can get out after a few hours. You can't stay. (If you suffer from depression, this is not for you. Stay far away from the edge of the pit.) Spending time in the pit can be like a mini-vacation. OK, a bad mini-vacation where it rains every day and the food is yucky because if you stay longer than that, your misery and pain can become an idol that sits higher on your priority list than God.

Rules of Pit Dwelling: First, you have to know and recognize you are going to visit the pit and ask a prayer warrior to pray for you while you are there. For example, I will say, "Ok, Kirsten I'm in the pit today. Having a little pity party for myself and rolling around in my "yuck," but I'm not planning on staying, redecorating and having cocktails. I need to sit in this for a while, feel it and embrace it. I'm coming out tomorrow after God and I work through some things, but please pray for me and call me tomorrow to make sure I'm out."

Rejoice with those who rejoice; weep with those who weep. Romans 12:15 (HCSB)

I don't want her to talk me out of going. I don't want her to tell me why I shouldn't go. I simply want her to pray for me and love me enough to make sure I climb out after the weeping. If you've never been in the pit, I envy you. If you have, I pray you can identify when you are in it and can climb out quickly after gaining strength through the Lord. If you ever visit the pit, I pray you understand that it's ok, you are only human, and God is beside you, but please ask others to pray for you while you are there and hold you accountable to climb out quickly.

We can go there, but we can't stay! We have to find the safest place to seek shelter, and that's not in a pit but the shelter of our Heavenly Father.

Whoever dwells in the shelter of the Most High will rest in the shadow of the Almighty. I will say of the Lord, "He is my refuge and my fortress, my God, in whom I trust." Psalm 91:1-2 (NIV)

This verse is a powerful reminder of the God we serve and the provision He promises those who seek and obey Him. So often, Satan will try to bind our hearts and minds with lies of shame, fear, distrust, guilt, anger, despair. He desires for us to feel all alone in our struggles, temptations, and lives. When we are isolated, the lies grow and have the ability to get so loud that everything else is drowned out. They overcome and overwhelm, leaving us with only a feeling of defeat. We can become isolated if we remain in the pit. Notice how Scott surrounded himself with family and friends during his time of need. They walked alongside him, encouraged him and no doubt prayed for him.

Satan strives to make us feel alone and vulnerable. He wants us to think we aren't good enough so that we don't dare to move forward from the past and climb out of the pit, BUT our God is cheering for us!

Resist him, standing firm in the faith, because you know that the family of believers throughout the world is undergoing the same kind of sufferings. 1 Peter 5:9

David penned Psalm 91 after Saul began hunting him to end his life. It's a miraculous story I hope you will read in 1 Samuel. In the end, God prevails and restores Saul's heart from the hatred it had been simmering in (1 Samuel 24). The verses from this Psalm are filled with awe and praise to God for delivering him from his enemy. For us, there are some marvelous reminders of the protection God promises if we are dwelling and abiding in Him.

Psalm 91:4—putting us under His wing
Psalm 91:5—gives us confidence so we will not fear
Psalm 91:11—promises us assistance from His angels
Psalm 91:14—promises to rescue and protect us IF we love Him.

He doesn't promise to remove us from the battle or the conflict, but if we are dwelling in Him, He promises protection. But how? Where do we start? How do we make it happen? Thankfully, He tells us over and over again in scripture.

Call to me and I will answer you and tell you great and unsearchable things you do not know. Jeremiah 33:3 (NIV)

So I say to you: Ask and it will be given to you; seek and you will find; knock and the door will be opened to you. Luke 11:9 (NIV)

If any of you lacks wisdom, he should ask God, who gives generously to all without finding fault, and it will be given to him. James 1:5 (NIV)

What should we do if we need wisdom, faith, healing, peace, courage, discipline? Ask! Just ask. There is no special form and no fee, merely ask with a willing heart.

PRAYER
Father, may the words of Psalm 91 that David penned so long ago penetrate our hearts in a new way today.

You who sit down in the High God's presence,
spend the night in Shaddai's shadow,
Say this: "GOD, you're my refuge.
I trust in you and I'm safe!"
That's right—he rescues you from hidden traps,
shields you from deadly hazards.
His huge outstretched arms protect you—
under them you're perfectly safe;
his arms fend off all harm.
Fear nothing—not wild wolves in the night,
not flying arrows in the day,
Not disease that prowls through the darkness,
not disaster that erupts at high noon.
Even though others succumb all around,
drop like flies right and left,
no harm will even graze you.
You'll stand untouched, watch it all from a distance,
watch the wicked turn into corpses.
Yes, because GOD's your refuge,
the High God your very own home,
Evil can't get close to you,

harm can't get through the door.
He ordered his angels
to guard you wherever you go.
If you stumble, they'll catch you;
their job is to keep you from falling.
You'll walk unharmed among lions and snakes,
and kick young lions and serpents from the path.
"If you'll hold on to me for dear life," says GOD,
"I'll get you out of any trouble.
I'll give you the best of care
if you'll only get to know and trust me.
Call me and I'll answer, be at your side in bad times;
I'll rescue you, then throw you a party.
I'll give you a long life,
give you a long drink of salvation!" Psalm 91 (MSG)

JAKE

I knew I was going to write about the life lesson learned from the short time we had Jake the Yellow Lab in our home. What I didn't realize was that a short story I wrote many years ago would fit so well...

PUPPY DOGS AND ICE CREAM

There once was a boy who listened when he was spoken to. Having been instructed to respect and learn from the adults in his life, he believed what they told him. For a very long time, he believed that life *wasn't* all puppy dogs and ice cream.

On a steamy Saturday morning in July, the boy and his father went to the barbershop for a haircut. He had almost finished one of the strawberry suckers that Wally the Barber had given him when he heard it on the radio. As they pulled into the garage, the sportscaster shared the news that the boy's NFL idol and friend of his family had passed away, just hours before.

While wailing away, face down on the bed in his room painted in team colors, his father approached. "Son, I know you loved him. He was very kind to you. But son, you need to know that life isn't all puppy dogs and ice cream. It simply isn't."

The boy thought about what his father said. He wiped away the tears and toughened up. *This is what men do*; he thought to himself. The quickness with which he got up from the bed, out of his room and on with life was acknowledged by a glance from his father as he walked down the hall. The boy wondered how much he believed what he had just been told, yet said nothing.

As he matured his way into young adulthood, the boy often thought about the day he had gotten a haircut and lost an idol and friend. The lesson of the moment seemed so harsh.

His time in college was filled with challenge and excitement. The future was here; the future he had worked so hard to create. He worked hard in the classroom. He earned a reputation as a respectable member of the campus community in the eyes of professors, members of the school administration and those for whom he worked at his on-campus jobs. All of this proved invaluable when his father lost his job.

"$25,000 per year, son," is what the portly, grey-haired Director of Financial Aid told the young man at a meeting just after he, too, received a call about the challenge the family was facing. "That is what it costs to go to this school. Did you know that, son?"

The young man nodded and shrugged slightly as if to say—*kinda*.

"Life isn't all puppy dogs and ice cream, you know this, yes?"

"Oh, yes sir, I know that very well," the boy replied.

"Son, this is a very expensive school, and your family can't afford to pay for it. That is the hard truth. Today, you are going to learn a lesson. How you have treated those around you and how hard you have worked to get good grades makes us want to keep you here. I'm not going to give you a puppy dog, but I guess you might feel like I've given you some ice cream today. We have expanded your financial aid dramatically, no strings attached."

The boy wondered how much he believed what he had just been told, yet said nothing. Surely there are conditions of this. I don't see any ice cream anywhere, he thought.

Moments like these built on each other as years passed and the boy became a man; the lack of hair on his head by age forty served as proof. Blessed he was with a beautiful wife, two very well-loved children, and a successful career.

In late April, just a month after blowing out what seemed to be an inferno on his birthday cake, the sudden loss of his father shook him to his core. An illness of just a few days had taken his father from his arms to the arms of the Father.

As he stood at the bedside, examining every inch of his father's face, head and perfectly combed hair in the quiet hospital room, words came to the son's lips he did not expect.

"Life isn't all puppy dogs and ice cream, is it dad?"

Since their life together was full of memories with their German Shepherd puppy dogs—three of them, in total—it seemed entirely fitting that one sat at attention at the head of the grave during the entire service, three days after his passing.

The days and weeks that followed were busy and sad. The boy had become a man, yet was often reminded of his time as a boy with his dad and their dogs. His wife and children witnessed the importance of those three big, strong dogs he had grown up with and the idea of getting one of their own was brought up.

"We can get one if you'd like, honey," his wife said, trying to hide the caution stirring in her head.

"Come on dad, let's get one," the kids said, over and over.

"But honey, I will say, it would be kind of neat to start our own family tradition," said his wife, with a wink.

"A Yellow Lab, I'm guessing?" the man said to his wife.

"Well, our first 'child' *was* a Yellow Lab, honey," she said with another wink, reminding him of the dog they had early in their marriage before children arrived on the scene.

A few months passed and the hope of getting a second dog had faded from the memory of everyone in the family, except for one.

We have a dog, he thought. *I was just emotional.* Their little twenty-pound fur ball was cute, but not quite the eighty-five-pound beast he had grown up with.

A quick peek at the Internet changed it all.

"I've lost my job and can't care for Jake during the last years of his life like I'd like to," said the posting that sought a new home for the awesome Yellow Lab.

The whisper from above seemed loud enough to be heard from coast to coast.

No matter that he weighs 100 pounds. Who cares that he is ten years old and has brutal arthritis. You can vacuum up the white hair off your cherry floors. Go get him, son. Take care of that beautiful dog in his waning years. Love on him like you did our dogs. You're doing a good thing for someone else. Life CAN be all puppy dogs and ice cream.

Jake the Yellow Lab, or "Jake the Great" as it read on his papers, fit into the family like a family fits into a minivan.

On a late summer evening, with the sun setting, the man took Jake for a slow and short walk. He had just finished a conversation with Jake's ten-year owner and had given an update as to how well Jake was doing, and how much his family was enjoying him.

As they meandered down the sidewalk, he got a giggle from the grin Jake exuded, even while hobbling painfully on the way back to his new home. The man couldn't help but be reminded of the grin on one of his German Shepherd's faces as he tore through a sand trap on the golf course where they used to take walks after the course had closed for the day.

It seemed only fitting to share a sacred after dinner treat with this dog that brought him so much joy after such sadness hit his family. The man reached his hand down and learned something new about his new friend—turns out, Jake likes Butter Pecan.

Life *can* be all puppy dogs and ice cream.

The End.

That was a sweet ending to a mostly true story that included the loss of my childhood idol and friend, my father's job and my father. Creative liberties and reality diverged a bit because, in truth, we ended up fostering the dog, returning him to his owner and having sadness enter our household again, way too soon after losing my dad.

Trust.

I worked hard to build it with Jake's owner when we spoke after I had seen his impassioned Craigslist post about his beloved dog. He had raised Jake from puppy to service dog. Their bond could never be broken even if they were living apart, which needed to happen due to an unfortunate series of events in his owner's life. Our first phone call had revealed that he lost his job and the love of his life then found a new love in alcohol and drugs. Since he lived alone, Jake was standing between his owner and rehab. He knew he needed help and Jake needed a home, which I was willing to provide.

I quickly learned that someone who is feeling like life is out of control is going to latch on to whatever and whomever he possibly can so he can take back some control. In this case, it was to have a long, ongoing conversation about where his dog would be living and how Jake would be treated. With as much respect, honesty and kindness I could muster, I told him the following:

I am a respected member of the community by way of a 15+ year career in a sales-related job
and,
I have written two inspirational books to serve others and have given many speeches and news interviews as well in support of those books
and,
I'm not letting you come to my house to see where Jake is going to live out of respect for my family's privacy and safety due to the demons you are currently battling
and,
you need to trust me.

The fact that he did not let me take Jake the first time I went to his apartment proved that Jake's owner did not appreciate the lack of control. The fact that I offered to drop him off at a well-known rehab facility on my way from his apartment to Jake's new home—my home—carried no weight with him, either. A call back a few days later proved to me that he was not only really, really ready to get better, but that he would now allow Jake to go with me.

Upon my return to his apartment, I was handed medicine, toys and a huge dog bed for this huge dog. In return, I handed Jake's owner a copy of both of my books along with another book I thought he might find helpful. I also left him with a promise to stay in touch, which led to a movie-script-worthy series of events that occurred after I fell in love with this sweet soul of a dog that I affectionately nicknamed, "Old Man."

I was so raw from losing my father just a couple of months earlier and saw this as a chance to fill a considerable gap that now existed in my life. In all honesty, I felt like I had been majorly gipped by God when I was not given any chance to care for my father before he passed away. He was still living on his own and, for the most part, taking care of himself. Then, in a matter of a few days, he was gone. I now had the opportunity to take care of an old man in his last days; this one just had two additional legs and a tail. Jake's condition was indeed that of an old man who needed taking care of; an initial exam by a Veterinarian on the second day we had him revealed a severe flea infestation, a hematoma on his ear flap from shaking his head due to itchiness from fleas (and whacking his ear on the table or whatever was nearby), severe arthritis and hip dysplasia. Ten years on this planet certainly did seem like seventy for this 100-pound bundle of Yellow Lab awesomeness. I fell head over heels for him and his snoring, smiling self.

A couple of months and almost two thousand dollars later, I found myself in tears having to give him back. The arrangement we had made to stay in touch proved to be a disservice to all. I felt like Jake's owner would benefit from the hope that he could, one day, get his dog back—that this would give him something to strive for, to live for. Instead, it provided a source of stress as well as an opportunity to try to control a situation he had proven he could not manage on his own. Phone calls, emails, and texts created drama, but drama I was willing to endure in hopes of a positive outcome for all (and fulfillment for myself that I could take care of an old man).

On the Friday of the Sandy Hook school shooting, I received an email from Jake's owner that broke the camel's back, "That's a nice looking Saab you've got. I drove by today to see if I could catch a glance at Jakey, but he wasn't outside."

Game over.

My heart started racing and my cortisol levels spiked. My fear for my family immediately replaced my need, want and desire to take this wonderful addition to our family through his golden years. After a few heated phone calls, arrangements were made for Jake's return to his owner who had not, unfortunately, been able to beat the demons. One additional call to a trusted friend whom I knew would say 'yes' to riding shotgun on the twenty-minute delivery trip and we were off.

'Unpleasant' is the word to describe the exchange that happened when Jake went home. After Jake's litany of *new* medicines, his toys, and his dog bed were laid outside the apartment, his leash was handed over, and my books were returned to me...unread...forcefully thrust against my chest with a threat added for good measure. While I've never been a fan of the saying, "No good deed goes unpunished," it immediately came to mind. Jake was now terminal due to an inoperable cancerous growth that had just appeared on his front leg, and this relationship was terminated as well.

I felt like I had just lost my dad. Again.

However, to this day, I am thankful for the opportunity to sneak into that dog's life.

To this day, I think about his owner and my sincere hope that he is thriving.

To this day, I believe that it is good that this whole thing ever happened.

Jake made me smile when I needed a source of smiles. He helped my kids see the love and emotion that a dog can bring to a family, to the point that we have since fostered multiple dogs in our home. The story of Jake told now and as it was unfolding, helps us to see God at work. People (with and without the last name 'Wittig') thought I was certifiably insane to bring home a ten-year-old, 100-pound dog that needed to be lifted in and out of a car, let alone one that came from a situation as this one did.

Why not?
If not me then who?
What's the worst that could happen?

Do it anyway. BGUD2PPL like my license plate says. It's cathartic to live differently than the norm, to step out and do stuff we may have always left to others to do.

We can all do well—and do well for others—if we listen to the whisper when it comes. I thought the whisper to take Jake was from my father; perhaps it was from The Father.

Mess to message: *Thank you, Jake and Jake's owner. I appreciate you allowing me into your lives and showing me what it's like to be a part of the incredible bond that can be shared between man and dog. My sincere hope is that you are both recovered, doing great and at peace, wherever you may be.*

† BLUEBERRY OR CHERRY PIE? †

What if Scott had let fear change the way his heart was leading him? How did he allow God's whisper of helping Jake stay above the noise of the complicated situation with Jake's owner? Since the owner never got treatment, was it all for nothing? Did Scott feel as if he had misunderstood God's nudge? How did he stay focused on the positives when it didn't turn out the way he wanted it to?

I always say, "You know it's God speaking when what He's asking you to do doesn't make any sense." Over the years, He has asked me to help a disabled stranger put on her shoes, torn me out of my comfort zone and placed me in public speaking, and even called us to another church when we believed we were right where we were supposed to be. If you have accepted Christ as your Savior and strive to follow His ways, consider all the times God has nudged you. How many times were those things 1) never what you would have chosen or expected 2) took you way out of your comfort zone, but 3) left you more blessed than before? I think Scott would agree to all three of those statements after his experience with Jake.

This is what the Lord said to me: "Go and buy yourself a linen undergarment and put it on, but do not put it in water." So I bought underwear as the Lord instructed me and put it on. Then the word of the Lord came to me a second time: "Take the underwear that you bought and are wearing, and go at once to the Euphrates and hide it in a rocky crevice." So I went and hid it by the Euphrates, as the Lord commanded me. Jeremiah 13:1-5 (HCSB)

OK, the Lord has placed a lot of things on my heart over the years, but He has never urged me to purchase underwear, wear it for a while and then hide it under a rock by the creek in our backyard. Who says the Bible isn't fun to read? But, let's not miss how obedient Jeremiah is when the Lord speaks to Him. This was undisputedly an unusual request, but Jeremiah never questioned why or what in the world for, He just followed the Lord's command. Where did that colossal faith come from? Did he even question God or go straight to the rocky crevice and bury the underwear? Do you remember a time God tugged at your heart to step out in faith and do something unexpected? Like Scott with the dog, maybe?

As we continue reading in Jeremiah, it says (v. 6-7) that "a long time later" the Lord tells him to return to the same spot where he hid the underwear and dig it up. Of course, Jeremiah finds what you would expect: old, dirty, stinky and maybe even decaying underwear full of holes that were of no use to anyone. Where is God going with all of this?

Then the word of the Lord came to me: "This is what the Lord says: Just like this I will ruin the great pride of both Judah and Jerusalem. These evil people, who refuse to listen to Me, who follow the stubbornness of their own hearts, and who have followed other gods to serve and worship—they will be like this underwear, of no use at all. Just as underwear clings to one's waist, so I fastened the whole house of Israel and of Judah to Me"—this is the Lord's declaration—"so that they might be My people for My fame, praise, and glory, but they would not obey. Jeremiah 13:8-11 (HCSB)

In these verses, God uses the dirty underwear to illustrate how useless the people who have turned from His ways are to Him and foretells of their ruin. But for us, this is a beautiful reminder to look for God in the ordinary. A reminder to listen to Him and follow His nudge and whispers even when they don't make sense. Just as Jesus used relatable stories and proverbs to teach His people when He walked this earth, God still uses our daily circumstances to teach and guide us, but we must trust Him. Learning to skip the why and what ifs and follow His lead is imperative. When we push God aside, refuse to listen to Him, and refuse to follow Him we are nothing more than dirty underwear and useless for His kingdom and drawing the hearts of others to Christ. I don't know about you, but I want to be like the elastic waist in that underwear that "clings" to my Heavenly Father and cut free of the world.

Who knew underwear could teach us so much?! I love our God!

Scott understood the value and impact of having Jake in his life even if only for a brief moment; he was able to see the blessings he received from the experience. What he may never know is the effect he had on Jake's owner. Scott's actions planted a seed of kindness. He may not have seen it watered, fertilized and sprouted, but it had been planted. That is all God needed from Scott at the time, and he listened.

It is vital to keep in mind that our plans don't always look the way God's plans do. They don't always turn out the way we expect, and they certainly don't end how we would choose sometimes, but they all fit into the story of life.

I'll never forget the night I learned this lesson from blueberry pie. I had a wonderful group of women over for an evening of fellowship and encouragement. Everything was fine until the time for dessert arrived, and we ran into a pie problem. My friend, who had been craving blueberry pie, bought what looked like and was labeled a blueberry pie. However, as we cut into the pie, it quickly became clear that wasn't blueberry at all, but cherry. She was devastated. As women, we can get like this over dessert! It's true.

Not wanting any disappointment that evening, I conspired with another friend who ran out to get her a blueberry pie. After that, we all got a good laugh about it as we enjoyed a little taste of both cherry and blueberry pie that evening. All the while, she was saying, "I know God will teach me something from the pie situation. I'll keep you posted." Oh, she's a woman after my own heart, always striving to learn and grow in God's ways. As promised, the next day she sent an email with the lesson God had placed on her heart.

She said, "Sometimes we are looking forward to and planning on the blueberry pie (what we want for our children, friends, life, family) but God is busy at work making them cherry pie (what He has planned). Rest in knowing either outcome is very sweet, but how pleasing it must be to Him to relish that cherry pie!"

After a week full of uncertainties concerning what path God desired for our daughter to follow concerning her education, I don't know if there was another person in the group that needed to hear those words more than I did. I was so grateful for the reminder that we should *always rejoice, pray without ceasing, give thanks in all circumstances; for this is the will of God in Christ Jesus for you.* 1 Thessalonians 5: 16-18 (HCSB)

However, this is an important reminder for all of us because even when we are uncertain and hurting there's always hope for those who trust and believe in Jesus. He took away the wrath of God we deserve for our sins and replaced it with grace. Grace is a gift that isn't deserved. We have been gifted grace, and that's reason enough to give thanks. If you haven't accepted Christ and His gift of grace and feel like you are ready to receive Him as your Lord and Savior, we have more information and a prayer at the end of the book you can pray to receive Him into your life and heart.

Answered prayers and life circumstances don't always look like what we thought they would, should or want them to be, but God is in the details. Scott certainly experienced this when it came to Jake. He didn't want to say goodbye to Jake that soon. He wanted Jake's owner to step up and take ownership of his addiction so he could recover. It doesn't happen the way we would choose sometimes, but we can't give up or give in. We must keep praying, keep trusting, keep rejoicing and keep thanking Him in every circumstance. In what situation could you do a little more praying, celebrating and praising?

Ask God to reveal the things in your heart that create an obstacle to trusting in His plan over yours, believing He is there for you and has the best story written for your life and those around you.

Search me, God, and know my heart; test me and know my concerns. See if there is any offensive way in me; lead me in the everlasting way. Psalms 139:23-24 (HCSB)

Maybe it's just me, but this verse can strike a bit of fear in me. My brain thinks, "Yikes, not sure I want God looking into my heart and testing it today. I'm not sure He would like what's in there." I mean there's some good stuff, but let's be real, it's not all sparkly clean in there. I'm sure there is trash I don't even realize is hanging around in there making things a little dusty and cluttered. Just to start: fear, pride, frustration, insecurity. What else? I'm sure I could keep adding to that list.

My mom isn't a "Type A" like me. Just looking in her office can give me the hives. She always talks about cleaning it up, but it never happens. We have done it together a few times, and it will stay that way for a few weeks; then it's right back to where she started. In her defense, I may have a super clean and organized office, but I hate weeding my flowerbeds. You won't find one weed in her flowerbeds!

My point in sharing about my mom and me is to make clear that cleaning and weeding a priority can be difficult. As we have seen in the previous chapters, God had been doing some serious weeding in Scott's heart, and Scott was growing in new ways. When we are in a time of pruning, there can be a lot to do; it can be dirty and hard work. It takes time, effort, discipline, and a willing heart to make it a priority. But when we do, the benefits are AWESOME! When my mom has a clean office, she loves it and enjoys using her office. When my plant beds are weeded, I enjoy sitting on my front porch so much more.

It's the same with God and our hearts! Asking God to search, examine, and investigate our hearts for discrepancies and fears can be scary. When I ask myself, "Why is fear your first response to this scripture/request?" I think there are several reasons.

1. I don't want God to think badly of me or that I can't handle it.
2. I know it will require hard work with God to work through the heart things with Him.
3. It's easier to tuck things away and keep moving forward than to stop and deal with them.

Ok, when I type all of my fears out, they don't seem very good or logical anymore. How about your fears? So, here is the truth about those irrational fears that popped up in my heart.

First, God already knows everything about me, my heart and loves me anyway. He also knows I can't handle anything without Him nor did He create me to. Plus, God doesn't judge. He extends mercy, forgiveness, and grace to all His children.

Second, yeah it's going to require some work, but don't all great things? Isn't that little bit of work, discomfort, and pruning worth the gift of eternal life, a whole heart and His glorious light in my life to share with others?

Third, everyone knows that tucking things away never gets you anywhere. It only holds you back. Plus, it's just letting Satan win, and for goodness sakes, I never want him to win!

Sometimes, we have to dig into the fear or our first instinctual feelings and ask ourselves why it's so scary, makes us angry or causes us anxiety. Why do we have a negative response? Once it's out in the open and we have processed the emotions, they shrink to the size of a sunflower seed compared to the glorious promises of our Creator, King, and Father. May His word continue to pierce our hearts and uncover any offenses so that we can continue to grow stronger in our faith and shine His great Light into the world.

PRAYER
Father, give us eyes to see and ears to hear the tasks you want us to pursue in your Name. Turn down the volume of this world and turn up the one to Your voice so when you call; we answer and act without delay. Give us a heart for Your people and may Your light burn so bright in us that there is no doubt it comes straight from Heaven. Give us courage and strength to follow your lead even when we can't make sense of the request. Please grant us peace when you pull us back, and we don't feel as if we have done all we can. Guide our hands, feet, and hearts as we seek to know and serve you daily. Amen.

SAM

Our family had lived in the same neighborhood for seven years. It was a cozy part of a larger subdivision that had no through streets and had a tight group of neighbors. When the time came to let some of those neighbors know that a sign was going up in the yard, it came clear that they had some anxiety—not only about losing us—but about the possibility that the new inhabitants would put up a fence, have barking dogs or be anti-social. A few days after we let the cat out of the bag, we went out to dinner with two couples we were very close with in the 'hood. With me as the designated driver, we had all ridden together to the restaurant. On the way home, a stop at the ATM was required since we all had babysitters waiting for us who were looking to get paid.

I'll never forget what happened next.

Sam, Brian and I got out of the car at the ATM and, as we were walking to get our cash, Sam stopped me and said, "What makes you so special that you get to be happy?" There are times in life when you are so psyched because you have just the right words to say back to somebody—this wasn't one of them for me. My jaw dropped. I stopped for a second and took it all in.

There we were, three educated, seemingly happy guys in our 40's and one of them says <u>that</u>? Our friends knew the reasons we were moving, with one of the big ones being money. We wanted to live with less and be able to live *on* less should things come together for me to be able to work for a non-profit, which would not provide nearly the income that a long-tenured banking career did.

The sentiment that Sam shared so honestly is shared by so many who are in careers they don't love and who are living lives that aren't fulfilling and don't make them happy. "What makes you so special and why do you get to be happy?" I believe we are all special and that there are things we can do to find happiness and purpose in our lives; we just need to be willing to do more than "the usual."

In *Holy It!*, I wrote about the importance of finding your "something bigger"—your thing in life that you were put here to do, that you're passionate about. It may come from something awesome or awful that has happened in your life. Mine came from walking alongside Ella's family as she fought the good fight against childhood cancer. That experience, followed by the sudden loss of my father and exposure to the good that organizations like Lighthouse do in this world, started a positive shift in the mindset, actions, and faith in and of our family, for which I am so thankful.

*

In his book *Outliers*, Malcolm Gladwell talks about all of the circumstances that go into a plane crash. In most cases, the crash is not due to one thing that went wrong—it's a bunch of things; a confluence of bad stuff that happens and leads to a bad ending. That's pretty much what happened to me in high school, but the ending wasn't as horrible as it could have been.

When I was a sophomore, I got dumped by a freshman. Right around that same time, my dad lost his job. That confluence of bad stuff led to me trying to kill myself twice. As I said, the ending wasn't as bad as it could have been. I'll take short and bald as compared to the alternative.

The biggest thing that almost led to my demise was my materialism and my inability to be happy with what I had. I always wanted more—and the best of "more"—but our family couldn't afford more or the best. Luckily, at that tender age, I learned that there were things about me that were special—having that knowledge was much more valuable than *stuff*. As an adult, helping your family come to that realization can be a pivotal point for all involved and, as we learned from Sam's comment at the ATM, can stir some emotions in those around you who may want to live with less stuff (and lower payments) as well.

Comparison is the thief of joy. You can't feel special if you're always comparing yourself to others—doing so will simply not bring happiness. Jeanne and I had this realization and, while throwing the sign in the yard of a home we loved (that was surrounded by neighbors we adored) was nothing short of emotional, the happiness that came from focusing on experiences instead of things was priceless. Perhaps the biggest benefit of this move—which put us a whopping one-mile away from the previous home—will be seen in our children as they grow older. Hopefully, they will not fall prey to "The Comparison Trap" (as Atlanta megachurch Pastor Andy Stanley calls it) that causes so many of us to live in "The Land of -ER"—"bigger...pricier...larger...prettier...shinier...wider...taller...

After finding Lighthouse, I felt so connected to it and learned the lesson of working toward a goal that involved serving others. Working for that ministry may never happen but, either way, I am fortunate to have found unbelievable clarity on what is truly important and worthy of our time, talent and treasure.

The thing is, it's not like we took a vow of poverty by downsizing—we went to a nice house, just one with less stuff and a lower mortgage payment. There is a passage in the bible that speaks to this mindset so well—it says, "Better one handful with tranquility than two handfuls with toil and chasing after the wind." (Ecclesiastes 4:6, MSG) Let us shoot for tranquility over toil and chase after passions instead of the wind.

Should you decide that such a change is what is best for your family, know this—it may feel like a risk. Hopefully, Journalist Linda Ellerbee's words will resonate with you as they did with me, "If you're taking a risk, what you are saying is, 'I believe in tomorrow, and I will be a part of it.'" Also, know that you will have naysayers and you will have cheerleaders. You will have "Sam's" who say things like, "What makes you so special that you get to be happy?" Sam's choice of words could easily put him in the naysayer category, but I choose to take them as constructive and call him a cheerleader, albeit in his own special, cynical-sounding way! Let us say together that we the people *are* special, and we *do* get to be happy. We have to listen when we hear the call to change. The people whom we think are calling us out might be the ones who ultimately support us, like Sam did when he helped us get a $12,000 donation to Lighthouse Family Retreat—the largest single donation I was able to obtain after two years of effort.

Mess to message: *A seemingly cynical comment from a good friend leads to perspective and encouragement for others, as well as a big donation for an awesome ministry. Thank you, Sam. Your willingness to be blunt and say it like it is has helped others in a very cool way.*

† HIGH PLACES †

How many hours of pillow talk and discussions over dinner had Scott, and his wife had before deciding to trust and follow God's lead to downsize? Was God's plan so clear that their fear was overshadowed or did they go in head first trusting God who often merely says, "Go!" and doesn't explain the when and how for some time? How did Scott harness the idols in his heart, so they were no longer a blockage for God to work through him?

No one can serve two masters. Either you will hate the one and love the other, or you will be devoted to the one and despise the other. You cannot serve both God and money. Matthew 6:24 (HCSB)

For the love of money is a root of all kinds of evil. Some people, eager for money, have wandered from the faith and pierced themselves with many griefs. 1 Timothy 6:10 (HCSB)

God must have known money and possessions were going to be one of the biggest idols we would have to overcome because money is mentioned over 800 times in the Bible and money and possessions over 2000. [iv] The first of the Ten Commandments (Exodus 20) is *"I am the Lord thy God! Thou shalt have no other gods but me!"*

The definition of an idol is: "A greatly loved or admired person, a picture or object worshipped as a god." As a

Christian, it's obvious we shouldn't have any golden cows, suns or oxen hidden in our closets that we pray to every night.

But, I want to point out that an idol is anything we allow to consume our thoughts, admiration, and love above our Heavenly Father. Scott recognized that one of his idols was materialism. The following idols are just the tip of the iceberg, but a great place to start checking because sometimes they are so deeply rooted, we don't even know they are there. Where you find idols, you find fear. These are some of the most common idols we struggle with.

1. **Our Spouse/Marriage** ~ When we idolize our spouse or marriage the fears that can exist are: What if he/she leaves me? What if they find someone else they love more? What if he/she doesn't think I'm pretty or smart enough now that I stay at home with our kids or lost my job?
2. **Our Children** ~ When we idolize our children the fears that can exist are: What if they hang out with the wrong crowd? What if they hear, see or do something morally wrong? What if they don't get a good job? What if they aren't good enough at sports or pretty enough to fit in with the crowd? What if they get hurt or sick?
3: **Our Image (social or physical):** When we idolize our image the fears that can exist are: What if everyone else looks better than me at the party? What if my spouse leaves me for someone younger, thinner, smarter? What if I don't get invited to the party and everyone else does? What if everyone else can participate and I can't?
4: **Financial Status**: When we idolize our finances the fears that can exist are: How will we pay the bills, send the kids to camp like their friends, go on vacation, or go out to eat with our friends? How will we fit in if we don't have the money to take part in things? Who will take care of and pay for me when I'm older if I don't save?

The sad but ultimate truth is that making these things (and whatever else we have on our list) idols doesn't mean we have more control over them. It doesn't mean we can protect them, make them perfect or maintain them. That is Satan's lie. His lies create a diversion for us. He deludes us into thinking that if we worry ourselves to death over these idols, we can control and protect them. Along the way, Satan is accomplishing his goal of keeping our eyes off of God.

But the truth is, no amount of fear or thought of control can lead to the protection or guarantee that everything will end up the way we want it to. The faucet of fear can only be turned off when God is our focus. When God is at our center, the rest that revolves around Him will fall into place. Maybe not the place we wanted, but His place and nothing stops His plan. God will carry out His will, with or without our peace and with or without our idols. I can promise only this—along the way, when things don't go the way we wanted them to go, happen when we wanted them to happen or transpire as quickly as we had hoped, it will only be His peace and love that will bring us comfort and faith so that fear doesn't overtake us. We can remain steadfast through trial and stormy gale when the Savior is our rock and compass.

Let's take a look at someone who had this concept under control.

Abijah died and was buried with his ancestors in the City of David. His son Asa became the next king.
For ten years into Asa's reign, the country was at peace.
Asa was a good king. He did things right in GOD's eyes. He cleaned house: got rid of the pagan altars and shrines, smashed the sacred stone pillars, and chopped down the sex-and-religion groves (Asherim). He told Judah to center their lives in GOD, the God of their fathers, to do what the law said, and to follow the commandments. Because he got rid of all the pagan shrines and altars in the cities of Judah, his kingdom was at peace. Because the land was quiet and there was no war, he was able to build up a good defense system in Judah. GOD kept the peace. 2 Chronicles 14:1-5 (MSG)

Bigger and better always seems to be the way the world judge's value and success. Who has the tallest buildings, biggest house, bank account or company? I adore how this scripture from 2 Chronicles speaks of Asa removing the pagan altars and "high places" of Judah. Asa loved God and knew that by following His ways and laws, it would lead to blessings of peace, rest and abundance.

"High places" were the places of worship that the people of Judah had created to glorify their false gods and idols. As Asa's predecessors found out, when we take the one true God, our Creator, and demote Him from the high place in our own lives, things tend to fall apart. Quickly, we see the benefits of rest, peace and blessings fall away from us when we remove God from the equation. Honoring anything or anyone above the one true God can have devastating effects that ripple through our lives.

I try to stop often and check my heart for idols. They can be so sneaky and slip in undetected! Stopping to ponder and pinpoint what has taken up residence in the high place, where only God should dwell, is vital to a strong relationship with our Father. Sometimes, without realizing it, I've placed finances, worry, fear, self or schedules over God. Reflecting daily on the condition of our hearts can help us serve God as Asa did and keep God in the appropriate place in our lives. Because when we do, even amid the most overwhelming obstacles and trials, we can count on strength, courage, and protection from the Lord. Just as Asa did when his army of 580,000 came up against an army of one million and cried out, *"Lord, there is no one besides You to help the mighty and those without strength. Help us, Lord our God, for we depend on You, and in Your name we have come against this large army. Yahweh, You are our God. Do not let a mere mortal hinder You."* 2 Chronicles 14:11 (HCSB)

I pray you will prayerfully consider the following questions:

1. When you need direction, discernment, strength, and courage, do you seek God or someone (or something) else?
2. Do you believe in your heart that no one besides our God should reside in the "high place" of your life?

I hope you can answer 'yes' to both these questions most of the days of your life, but if you can't, please know that through prayer, discipline, and study God will defeat the idols that have taken up residence of your "high place." He desires to be your guide, protector, and comforter. Every single day is a battle to keep God in our high place, but He can break through the darkness with His light and win the fight.

Woe to those who go down to Egypt for help and who depend on horses! They trust in the abundance of chariots and in the large number of horsemen. They do not look to the Holy One of Israel and they do not seek the LORD's help. Isaiah 31:1 (NIV)

I realize these passages describe the fact that God's people were relying more on other countries and their resources for protection than they were God, but it made me realize once again how often we are just like Israel in our personal lives. Couldn't this verse also read:

Woe to those who turn to shopping, busyness and depend only on themselves. They trust only in themselves and the abundance of material things instead of looking to God for provision and protection. They build up earthly treasures instead of Heavenly ones. Woe to those who have forgotten to honor the ways and laws of the Lord and have allowed their hearts to be swayed by earthly desires.

That makes it a little more personal, doesn't it? How often do we skip the most critical step when faced with daily decisions big and small? How often do we allow pride to overtake our hearts, causing us to fail to seek God's desires above our selfish desires? Yikes, right?! I feel the conviction falling all over my heart. Scripture is a powerful and bold reminder that we must turn from other idols and only serve God. Repentance is non-negotiable! It's a must! The Lord alone is the only one who can save us, redeem us and complete us.

Woe to those of us who forget to seek the face of God daily. That's where Jesus comes in. He steps into the gap for us so that when we forget, there is still hope, mercy, and grace. The blood of Christ that was shed for us on the cross so long ago gives us access to forgiveness so we can be reconciled back to God with a simple, but humble request—Father, forgive me, I have sinned.

Scott began his story once the decision to move had already been made. Consider all the months of prayer and discussion he and his wife must have had weighing their options, considering their sacrifices and listening to be sure they were following God's lead. I am not going to sugar coat this! We will struggle for the rest of our days with releasing control of our lives and stomping the idols that creep in, but I pray God opens our eyes to our obstacles and continues to tug at our hearts, so we draw closer to Him and rest in Him more fervently every day.

I wonder when the moment hit that Scott was able to say, "I choose You, Father. I chose You over the world, and I would rather count pennies my whole life than lose You and the indescribable peace that you offer me in the good times and the bad. I choose your plan over mine and look forward to seeing the fruit of your labor through me."

We have heard many times, "Let go and let God," but do we ever heed the advice? Think of all the benefits we would receive if we would do as this saying suggests and let God in. Let Him in to heal the pain, take the place of something worldly or simply find rest in His presence and many blessings. God can come in and sweep out all the idols with one breath if we invite Him to. Just like a plumber would never come into your home and repair your broken garbage disposal unless you called to schedule his services, God will not force Himself into your life and clean up the mess without an invitation. And unlike a plumber, His service is free so what do you have to lose? What are you waiting for?

Jesus looked at them and said, "With man, this is impossible, but not with God; all things are possible with God." Mark 10:27 (NIV)

It is impossible for us to change our hearts without God's help. I urge you to search your heart for the things you have been holding on to but need to let go of. Go to God with the pain, hurt, anger, fear, guilt, embarrassment, stress, and worry. Place it at the foot of the cross.

We can't hide our thoughts and feelings from God. He knows us better than we know ourselves. Whether it's an addiction, a "worldly" idol, an impure thought, habit or lack of faith, we all have something we aren't proud of and would like to hide. The paradox is that the one we try to hide from and the one who loves us the most is the one we can never hide from. God knows our hearts and minds better than we know ourselves, and He is the only one who can make it pure again.

If we had forgotten to pray to our God or made fools of ourselves with store-bought gods, wouldn't God have figured this out? We can't hide things from him. No, you decided to make us martyrs, lambs assigned for sacrifice each day. Psalm 44:20 (MSG)

What if we used all the energy it took to hide from God and others and put it towards becoming better disciples of Christ? What if we allowed God's strength and power to reign in us? What if we dwelled on his word daily so we had God's direction and peace so instead of hiding from Him we allowed Him to protect and hide us from our enemies and the evil of this world? God has plans to "prosper us not to harm us" (Jeremiah 29:11) His plans are "immeasurably more than we could ever imagine" (Ephesians 3:20). I pray we can stop hiding and place it all on God's altar so that we don't miss out on the plans he had for us before we were created. Imagine how our lives would change, our faith would blossom and our trust would grow if we let God get a hold of our hearts.

God is bedrock under my feet, the castle in which I live, my rescuing knight. My God—the high crag where I run for dear life, hiding behind the boulders, safe in the granite hideout; my mountaintop refuge, he saves me from ruthless men. 2 Samuel 22:2 (MSG)

Invite Him in, He'll kick the idols and ways of the past to the curb, and your heart will be light and free to experience Him and His word in a new and amazing way. God will reveal Himself to you in ways you never imagined. Wouldn't it feel good not to have to hide anymore?

But how do we make it happen? Like Scott's decision didn't happen overnight, our transformation can't happen instantly either. We need a game plan.

Right now –
- Look at your calendar and block off 20 minutes in your week that you will spend with God. Maybe it's right now.
- Make yourself a promise that you will take this seriously and guard the time on your calendar with God just like you would for your hair appointment, pedicure, basketball game or girl's/boy's night out!
- Pick a scripture that touches you or has been in your weekly devotion. If you can't think of any on your own, look through the chapters of this book for some or use the ones I list on the next page. No excuses.

During your time with God –
- Sit in a quiet spot.
- Read the scripture you have chosen or that God has led you to.
- Close your eyes, reflect on His words, be still, listen for His whisper.

What it will do for you –
- I pray it brings you closer to God, that it allows you to hear His whisper, renews your mind and begins to teach you that being still is ok. This world tells us that, to be worth anything, we have to move all the time. That we have to have it all, gain it all and strive to be like everyone else. It says, our God isn't enough that we have to do it ourselves. But that is a lie. God tells us over and over in scripture to be still, keep our eyes on Him and trust in His ways.

What now?
- Consider putting this meeting with God on your calendar every week. My prayer is that as you do this you begin to desire more and more of this stillness with Him and the meetings begin to happen daily instead of weekly.

Scripture Ideas:

Finally, be strong in the Lord and in his mighty power. Put on the full armor of God, so that you can take your stand against the devil's schemes. For our struggle is not against flesh and blood, but against the rulers, against the authorities, against the powers of this dark world and against the spiritual forces of evil in the heavenly realms. Therefore put on the full armor of God, so that when the day of evil comes, you may be able to stand your ground, and after you have done everything, to stand.
Ephesians 6:10-13 (NIV)

LORD, be gracious to us! We wait for You.
Be our strength every morning
and our salvation in time of trouble. Isaiah 33:2 (HCSB)

He will never be shaken.
The righteous man will be remembered forever.
He will not fear bad news;
his heart is confident, trusting in the LORD.
His heart is assured; he will not fear.
In the end he will look in triumph on his foes. Psalm 112:6-8
(HCSB)

PRAYER

Father, give us a thirst for you that can never be quenched. Dust off the cobwebs and pull the door open to our hearts so your saving grace can flow in and flush out any idols we have put on high places. We need you and desire to have you dwell within us so we can access the clarity and courage it takes to turn away from the "Treasures on earth, where moths and vermin destroy, and where thieves break in and steal." Keep our eyes on you as we seek to find you and pray as you teach us in Matthew 6:5-15 (MSG), "Our Father in heaven, Reveal who you are. Set the world right; Do what's best— as above, so below. Keep us alive with three square meals. Keep us forgiven with you and forgiving others. Keep us safe from ourselves and the Devil. You're in charge! You can do anything you want! You're ablaze in beauty! Yes. Yes. Yes." Amen.

KEVIN

"**I**t's all bullshit."
Those were the words that started our meeting.

I looked forward to meeting Kevin McDonald after hearing so many good things about him. I think I was admiring a picture of him shaking hands with a Senator when Kevin greeted me in his conference room with those words. I can't remember for sure, though, because the walls of that conference room were covered with pictures of Kevin with political figures…beside framed community, state and national awards…beside framed newspaper articles touting his good works. I remember thinking if you don't do things for attention, you'll never have to act surprised when you get it. Kevin surely didn't do any of his work for attention; his comment about it all being BS proves it.

All BS? Surely not. Kevin is no joke. He'd tell you, however, that it's not about him; it's about what he started.

Kevin gives props to Mimi for what he started. I had read about the little pipsqueak of a woman who began the Delancey Street Foundation, Mimi Silbert. She has run one of the most successful rehabilitation organizations in the world for over 40 years. Based in San Francisco, California, Delancey Street is a "self-help organization for substance abusers, ex-convicts, homeless and others who have hit bottom." The organization is renowned for teaching life skills to people with no hope by way of work, *hard* work. The folks who are lucky enough to be remanded to Delancey Street (instead of prison) work hard as they run a moving company, a restaurant, a Christmas tree business, and a thrift store, just to name a few. The moving company is the highlight and turning point for many who go through the program because, as Kevin says, "They get to see something start and finish every single day."

Kevin found out about Delancey Street from a guy in a black gown that might well have been his Priest but was, instead, a judge in the courtroom Kevin found himself in regularly. An addiction to drugs and alcohol led to many petty crimes as he attempted to afford his addictions. Had he not landed at Delancey Street, he surely would have landed on the street, which is why Kevin says it was the best thing that ever happened to him.

After working extremely hard to break his bad habits by way of working on a moving truck and in the many other businesses that the foundation runs, Kevin graduated and found himself returning the favor by way of working closely with Mimi Silbert to run Delancey Street. After many years with Mimi, Kevin struck out on his own to start TROSA (Triangle Residential Options for Substance Abusers, Inc.) in Durham, North Carolina. Just as all the accolades in the conference room extoll, TROSA is a renowned and award-winning example of social entrepreneurship. TROSA serves male and female substance abusers in a very similar fashion to Delancey Street, through vocational training as well as counseling, mentoring and leadership training. It is quite the journey from the intake office to living in your own apartment outside of the TROSA residence halls, a journey that teaches:

- The importance of honesty—the movers will hand you a penny if they find it on the floor in the home or office they are moving for you.
- Giving—TROSA residents live by the creed "Each one teach one."
- Hope—a constant reminder is alongside them daily by way of graduates who return as counselors and employees of the organization.

"Do for others, for others will do for others as a result" were the words that popped into my head when I heard about the number of graduates who stay, or return, to help.

On the day I sat with this humorous and awesome human, Kevin gave me a great laugh when he said this about raising money for his non-profit, "I learned how to fundraise without a gun." Some of Kevin's words can seem to come out like a gun, to the point where the internationally acclaimed Fuqua School of Business at Duke University (which sits in TROSA's backyard in Durham) had to re-write their procedures for the times that Kevin presented as a guest lecturer. The re-write ended up having to be signed by the students, though, not Kevin.

You see, while his words may be inflammatory and harsh to the students as he calls them out for their first-world complaints (with the use of profanity as needed), their value is infinitely more important; the students had to sign a form to confirm that they would not complain to the administration about their feelings getting hurt or about being offended. Kevin's message that comes from his mess is just that valuable to our future leaders.

The two biggest takeaways from my time with Kevin:
1. "Talk about your freakin' feelings."
2. Life is about giving not taking.

If I heard this rough and tumble dude say the word "feelings" once in our hour-long conversation, I heard it twenty times. To a fault, I've always been a pretty open book, but I'm not sure I've talked about my feelings quite to the level that you do if you are a TROSA resident. The expression of your feelings is what makes you a human being instead of an addiction machine. It lets out what is all pent up and can easily lead to angry outbursts with bad endings. Letting out feelings builds friendships because it humanizes us to others who may share those same feelings.

The second takeaway (Kevin's statement about giving) hit home with me, to the point where I made the word "Give" my one-word filter for the next year (rather than a New Year's resolution). Give hope. Give money. Give time. Give your story. Give, give, give. The rewards of giving are far more plentiful than any gains from taking.

The last note from my conversation with Kevin says, "Doesn't read much or exercise." I guess not; the dude is too busy changing the world for 500+ people a year.

Mess to message: *Thank you, Kevin. By taking time out of your schedule for a guy you don't know, you provided this author with valuable words about redemption. You came out from under your own "black cloud of doom" and showed us the light of what can be.*

† RECYCLED †

I wonder if Kevin ever, in his wildest dreams, considered how God could take his past flaws and sins and turn them into something beautiful? Did he ever doubt he was worthy of God's love and forgiveness? Did he question why God would choose Him after all he had done in his past? How did he overcome the doubt and embrace God's bold plan for his life?

The potter's story from Jeremiah 18 came to mind after reading about Kevin's story of redemption.

This is the word that came to Jeremiah from the LORD: "Go down at once to the potter's house; there I will reveal My words to you." So I went down to the potter's house, and there he was, working away at the wheel. But the jar that he was making from the clay became flawed in the potter's hand, so he made it into another jar, as it seemed right for him to do. Jeremiah 18:1-4 (HCSB)

God used this illustration from verses 1-4 to show Jeremiah how He could change His mind and relent from punishing the House of Israel if they would turn from their evil ways. But for each of us, this is a beautiful reminder that when we start down the wrong path, we can always return back to God. If we allow Him into our hearts and lives, He can make something new out of us and restore the broken situation. After all, each of us are "flawed pots," made great only by the Maker's hands.

When we allow Him to shape and mold our hearts, desires, and minds, He can make us into beautiful works of art.

The word of the LORD came to me: "House of Israel, can I not treat you as this potter treats his clay?"—this is the LORD's declaration. "Just like clay in the potter's hand, so are you in My hand, house of Israel. At one moment I might announce concerning a nation or a kingdom that I will uproot, tear down, and destroy it. However, if that nation I have made an announcement about turns from its evil, I will relent concerning the disaster I had planned to do to it." Jeremiah 18:5-8 (HCSB)

Think about it, without God as our compass our lives will take on a flawed form. As I look back on the days in my life where I had put God aside and lived for my desires and pleasure, it was so shallow and filled with pride, selfish envy, temporary satisfaction, and sin that no one would have ever been able to recognize my Creator in me. Finally, God broke through. He took my warped clay and turned me into something new and magnificent. Yes, I still have scars, but He has made them beautiful. So beautiful that they are now a part of my story that I can use to share the gospel with others. Can you imagine the parts and pieces of Kevin's story that he can share with others who face the same struggles he did at one time? The challenges, obstacles, despair, victories, and successes are all woven into the thread of God's grand design for his life.

I'm not sure where you are today. Maybe you still feel like a flawed pot, or perhaps you have turned yourself over to the Creator for some modifications. The good news is that it's never too late. Whether you need to turn your entire life back over or just your sin from the day, the Master potter awaits your willing heart and can turn your flaws into something beautiful for His plan. He can take our trash and recycle it into the treasure of a lesson or new opportunity. He can take what once seemed useless and make it useful in ways we could never fathom.

God's kingdom is like a treasure hidden in a field for years and then accidentally found by a trespasser. The finder is ecstatic—what a find!—and proceeds to sell everything he owns to raise money and buy that field. Matthew 13:44 (MSG)

Recycle means to extract useful material. God is in the recycling business. Not in the recycling of plastic, paper, and cardboard, but the recycling of sin, disappointment, betrayal, fear, deception, and heartbreak. When I consider all my past mistakes, the trials that my friends and I have faced and endured, the messes and devastation sin has caused in my own life and the lives of those I know, I can see God at work in the midst of it all. He is recycling the hurt, extracting the useful material and the lessons and using it for His glory; all to draw us closer to Him. To trust in Him more and lean on His understanding more than our own and experience life more fully by doing so. Kevin's story is an incredible example of God's recycling capabilities.

This third I will put into the fire; I will refine them like silver and test them like gold. They will call on my name and I will answer them; I will say, 'They are my people,' and they will say, 'The LORD is our God.' Zechariah 13:9 (HCSB)

God turns trash into treasure! He uses mistakes and trials to refine us! To purify and perfect us. When we allow God in to do His work:

- Past mistakes turn into testimonies that draw others to Christ.
- Trials break down walls around our hearts that hinder us from hearing God's whisper.
- Weary and broken hearts turn into fertile ground where God can do His best work.
- Our weakness becomes God's mighty strength.

One of my favorite cards by Emily McDowell[v] reads, "In Japan, broken objects are often repaired with gold. The flaw is seen as a unique piece of the object's history, which adds to its beauty. Consider this when you feel broken."[vi] It's such a beautiful image of how God can recycle our brokenness into something worthy, meaningful and lovely.

Yes, I would say that our Lord and Savior is the ultimate recycler. He is undoubtedly able to turn all the trash we make out of our lives into treasure if we seek Him and allow Him to penetrate our hearts with His great love and forgiveness. God is willing and able, but sometimes we get in the way because of our doubt, fear, and unwillingness to trust in His mercy. For years of my life, I felt unworthy of being a part of God's plan and sharing His good news because I didn't grasp the deep love and total forgiveness He offers. I felt this way because I had only listened to what everyone else said about God instead of picking up the Bible to discover it myself.

When we doubt ourselves and wonder why God would choose such an unworthy servant to be a part of His great plan, we can look to the scriptures for encouragement. The Bible never ceases to inspire me as I read about and discover all the average, fragile and "normal" people God has called through history to accomplish His most amazing feats. First, there was Moses who said to the Lord when He called on him, *"Who am I that I should go to Pharaoh and bring the Israelites out of Egypt?"* Exodus 3:11

God wanted His people released from slavery and called on Moses to make it happen by going and talking to the Pharaoh who held them captive. Moses said to the Lord, *"Please, Lord, I have never been eloquent—either in the past or recently or since You have been speaking to Your servant—because I am slow and hesitant in speech."* Exodus 4:10 (HCSB)

I wonder if Kevin has ever felt as Moses did? I know I have. There have been more times than I would like to admit that I've said to the Lord, "Are you sure you have the right person?" I struggled with writing in school, public speaking used to be one of my biggest fears and let's not even talk about my past! Whew! This unworthy servant joins the ranks of so many others that came before.

Then there was Gideon, who after the Lord handed over the Israelites to Midian for seven years of captivity, called upon him to deliver the Israelites once again.

And he said to him, "Please, Lord, how can I save Israel? Behold, my clan is the weakest in Manasseh, and I am the least in my father's house." Judges 6:15 (ESV)

God continued His pattern and chose Gideon who was weak and young. It doesn't stop with Gideon—throughout the Bible from Genesis to Revelation; God does this. We haven't even gotten to David who defeats Goliath (1 Samuel 14). God uses the weak to lead the strong. As my kids would say, "It's how He rolls." Through our weakness and submission to Him, He can do a great work in us and through us for His glory. I dare say, in ways we would have never imagined or asked.

But he said to me, "My grace is sufficient for you, for my power is made perfect in weakness." Therefore I will boast all the more gladly of my weaknesses, so that the power of Christ may rest upon me. For the sake of Christ, then, I am content with weaknesses, insults, hardships, persecutions, and calamities. For when I am weak, then I am strong. 2 Corinthians 12:9-10 (ESV)

Be assured that if God calls you, He will equip you. You can see this in Kevin's story. Consider where he began and how God delivered him. Don't believe your past is too broken, your courage too fragile or that you don't have what it takes to serve our Lord. He is calling each of us in one way or another to share our faith, to be the light in this dark world and to love our neighbor as ourselves. Will you trust? Will you follow His lead?

PRAYER

Father, today we ask that you enter our hearts and lives. That you take all that is flawed within us and shape it into something new and beautiful. Take our sins, doubts, fears, and shame and cover them with your love and grace. Mold us and guide us into the children you always desired for us to be. Teach us to lean on You and to trust in Your grand plans for us. To know that you never leave us or forsake us. May we be Your light in this dark world and never pass up an opportunity to share our story and your great love with each person you place in our path. Amen.

DAN

If your nickname from your friends who have kids is "The Kid Whisperer," you are pretty darn likely to want to have kids. Dan definitely fell into that category. Fortunately for him, his four-year friendship with Kelly morphed into a serious relationship. They were engaged after less than a year of dating and Dan was headed toward the opportunity he was built for, being The Kid Whisperer to his own children.

Cancer delayed that plan just as it completely derails so many others.

The courtship and engagement had been as fun as anyone would hope. Yet, just after Kelly said 'yes' and well before she said 'I do,' her father got a very grim cancer diagnosis. Her relationship with her father was strong, and dad had been the glue that held the family together as mom came unglued regularly due to her ongoing battle with alcoholism. The loss of Kelly's father just three weeks before she was to marry Dan led to a challenging period and an incredibly awkward wedding reception; it would seem that the alcoholism gene flipped its switch inside of Kelly on what was to be one of the happiest nights of her life. She had entirely too much to drink and was embarrassing herself with lewd comments and immature behavior. Moments after Dan and Kelly became one; they split apart as Kelly was taken home prematurely from their reception by a caring, yet embarrassed family member. Their beginning marked the beginning of their end.

As they settled into their new life together, Dan hoped that he could help his new wife navigate through the grief of losing her father. Kelly's world had changed so dramatically in such a short period that she found it overwhelming and unbearable. The unraveling came quickly by way of being fired from her job and a DUI (which Dan soon learned was not her first, but her third). The newlyweds found themselves suffering from the "one-thing-after-another" syndrome, and Dan felt helpless. His anxiety issues that initially manifested themselves in his 20's had been dormant but came roaring back as Kelly's drinking continued unabated. Financial challenges ensued to the point where the vacation home they had purchased in hopes of having a cathartic place to get away from life's harsh realities became their primary home. They had found out quickly that they would not be counting on two regular incomes but Dan's income only, and lost their home to foreclosure.

As Dan felt more and more helpless by not being able to curb his bride's heavy drinking, he helped Kelly get into counseling and, eventually, into rehab. Dan learned a lot about rehab and, unfortunately, that rehab would beget rehab. The counselors taught Kelly how to stay away from alcohol while the other addicts taught her how to play the prescription game to get painkillers. When she went to rehab the second time, the counselors taught Kelly how to stay away from painkillers while the other addicts taught her how to use over-the-counter cold medicine to numb the pain of her suffering. The vicious cycle played out over and over.

When you are living with—and trying to love—someone who is fighting such a battle, you find yourself desperately wanting to celebrate battles won. Each time Kelly got out of rehab, a high occurred in their marriage. There was hope for Kelly and Dan. Everything was going to be ok after all. She was going to beat this. After discharge from the first rehab stint came the first child, and two children (twins) came after the second stint. Over and over they shared elation, then feelings of helplessness. Dan felt like a single parent for much of their marriage and Kelly made attempts at making him a permanent single parent more than once not only with her absenteeism but legal custody challenges as well.

Friendships were lost. Relationships with family were fractured. The dog was even involved as *his* pain meds even proved to be fair game. The breaking point for Dan came in front of counselors when he gave Kelly the final ultimatum. He could not have their children at risk any longer, a position they had been put in multiple times by Kelly's addiction. Divorce came with a diagnosis—not only was Kelly addicted, but she was also afflicted with bipolar and borderline personality disorders. For twelve years Dan thought his fight was against her addiction, but it was also against two other dark demons. The life he thought many women would die for, which included three beautiful and healthy children, was not one Kelly was meant to live.

"God puts people in our path because it's part of our journey to learn from each other." Those were Dan's words when I asked him why he thought this all went down the way it did. He believes that he was the one to be in Kelly's life at the time of her unraveling so she could benefit from his patience, self-control and ability to forgive; all traits he knew he had, he just expected them to be more needed when he had the dad hat on, not the husband one.

With his panic attacks gone and a girlfriend from years past, Kristen, now happily back in his life as his wife, Dan is focused forward on what is good—his relationship with his kids being extremely high on the good scale. Forming a tight bond built on love and trust had been a necessity as he, essentially, single-parented his three children in their youngest years. That connection is now his driving force in many ways.

Dan is focused on being a great dad and helping other dads do the same thing. Although he was the hero to his kids when he filled in for their often missing-in-action mother, he found that the books he was reading to them did not reflect the same. Dads were not regularly portrayed as the parent who came to the rescue when there were boo-boos and breaks. He found that, in many books, dads were not portrayed at all—they were notably absent. Dan is seeking to change that by way of a book series with 'dad' as the main character, a series for which he already has twenty-one stories prepared.

These stories are designed to help dads see how it is possible to truly connect with their kids, even if they only have a couple of hours a day to make that connection. The books come from the best place—truth and reality—as they are all based on experiences and adventures that Dan has shared with his children. He is living his life with Kristen and his children purposefully. Dan continues to challenge himself and has found a way to create accountability by way of a Facebook page called "Daddy Provides." He uses this page as a way to show other dads how to get creative with their dad-kid activities.

After being tagged as "The Kid Whisperer," perhaps Dan found himself future tripping to the time when he could be that to his children. How wonderful that he has traded Kelly's highs and his resultant lows for the elixir that *is* the present and he is using it to the good of others, for which dads like me are very thankful.

Mess to message: *Thank you, Dan. Your ability to fight through your own battle after trying to help Kelly fight hers has provided us with a story that can influence lives for years to come.*

† WAIT AND PERMISSION †

I wonder how many hours Dan spent praying Kelly would be healed from her addictions? Did he feel abandoned by God during those years when the struggles seemed to outweigh the victories? How did he survive the years of waiting until resolution came and God's plan made it right?

Dan's story made me think of how difficult waiting for answers, relief, healing, and restoration can be. It also reminded me of Psalm 25.

Make Your ways known to me, Lord; teach me Your paths. Guide me in Your truth and teach me, for You are the God of my salvation; I wait for You all day long. Psalms 25:4-5 (HCSB)

I can't help but see the word "*wait*" in this scripture highlighted, in bold script and flashing as I read over its beautiful words. "Wait" can become the theme of our lives during certain stages, challenges or prayer requests. I have certainly been there. Those times when each prayer or request in which I seek the Lord, the answer is "wait." Wait! Wait! Wait! Wait for the answers, wait for others to respond, wait to hear God's voice, wait for others to take action. It can be exhausting and feel very isolating.

Waiting for friends to be healed, addictions to be broken, marriages to be restored, love to fill a heart that has gone cold, children who have gone prodigal to return home, and simply direction on next steps in life can feel daunting and depressing.

I've had to remind myself over and over again:

Love the Lord your God, walk in all His ways, and remain faithful to Him. Deuteronomy 11:22 (HCSB)

The Rock—His work is perfect; all His ways are entirely just. A faithful God, without prejudice, He is righteous and true. Deuteronomy 32:4 (HCSB)

For He will give His angels orders concerning you, to protect you in all your ways. Psalms 91:11 (HCSB)

If you search the Bible, you will find the word "wait" over 120 times. I know I'm not the only one God has told and tells to "wait." In fact, reading back through Scripture, God reminded me that more often than not, the faithful are asked to wait.

Consider this:

Noah had to trust and wait for the rain and then the dove in Genesis.

In Numbers, Moses told his people to wait until he heard from the Lord and returned to them.

In Ruth, both Ruth and Naomi labored in the fields while waiting for God's final plan and the saving grace of Boaz.

Joseph had to wait in bondage and prison before becoming the King's first in command and restoring the family that sold him into slavery.

David had to wait and undergo loads of persecution before fulfilling his God-ordained destiny as leader of his people.

In Luke and the other gospels, God's people waited for the Savior. They even thought their Savior might be John the Baptist before Jesus arrived on the scene. And, the disciples had to wait three days before the reality of the resurrection occurred.

In Acts, the church had to wait for the Holy Spirit to descend upon them after Jesus's ascension into Heaven.

Even now, we are still waiting for our Savior's glorious return to bring us all into His loving arms for eternity.

Wait.

Now, like each of us, Dan can add his name to the list of expert "waiters." However, I believe there is a vital truth Dan must have clung to in his years of waiting. God is worth the wait! His plan is worth the wait. Yes, in this lifetime there is going to be a lot of waiting. What if we could shift our focus back to the wonder of the wait and the glorious riches that can come after the wait is over. Now, let's be real. It isn't easy to praise God and thank him for our challenges, trials, and mess, but if we can step back from it and lift our eyes to Him for even a brief moment, we will remember who He is, was and always will be. God is a loving Father who never sleeps nor slumbers and will not leave our side. (Psalms 121:3-4)

Wait for the Lord; be strong and courageous. Wait for the Lord. Psalm 27:14 (HCSB)

We wait for Yahweh; He is our help and shield. Psalm 33:20 (HCSB)

The Lord is good to those who wait for Him, to the person who seeks Him. Lamentations 3:25 (HCSB)

However, even after the wait is over and the sun comes up, we sometimes discover the desires of our hearts don't come to fruition. It was our plan, but not God's. The blueprints of our lives don't always get built out the way we planned or prefer. Look at these words from the book of Luke. What Jesus says to Simon Peter during the Last Supper and before He is crucified can easily be passed over because we are so focused on Simon

Peter's betrayal and the death of Jesus, but let's take a close look at what Jesus says about the power of permission.

"Simon, Simon, behold, Satan demanded to have you, that he might sift you like wheat, but I have prayed for you that your faith may not fail. And when you have turned again, strengthen your brothers." Peter said to him, "Lord, I am ready to go with you both to prison and to death." Jesus said, "I tell you, Peter, the rooster will not crow this day, until you deny three times that you know me." Luke 22:31-34 (ESV)

Did you see it? Satan asked if he could test Peter's faith and sift him as wheat. Crazy, right? Ever been through a time (maybe it is now) in your life where you felt as if you were put through the grinder or sifted? We know Dan's story, but I bet you have your own. We all do. Satan has to ask permission, but when he receives it, don't miss out on a breathtaking truth.

Jesus says this, *"But I have prayed for you, Simon, that your faith may not fail."*

Jesus, the Son of God, prayed for Simon just as He stands in the gap to cover our sin from God and He prays for us. Jesus prays for you and for me every time we are enduring a trial, feel as if we can't take one more step or seem to have lost all hope. Jesus prays for us! I wonder if Dan felt God upholding him in the wait and even when the answer to his prayer of healing for Kelly didn't happen?

You may be thinking what thousands of others have asked, "Why does a loving God allow His children to suffer heartache and pain?" I get it. But as hard as I have tried to find it in scripture, there is nowhere that says being a Christian makes life perfect, painless and blessed all the time. This is just one of the many reasons I believe the Bible is true, accurate and inspired by God. Yes, written by human hands but full of fact and wisdom (2 Timothy 3:16-17). Think about it; mankind is usually looking for the easy way out, so it's difficult for me to imagine we would write this story without adding, "Follow Jesus and your life will be perfect and blessed for all your days."

For one more example that shows Satan needs permission, take a look at these verses from Job that support this idea:

> *One day when the angels came to report to GOD, Satan, who was the Designated Accuser, came along with them. GOD singled out Satan and said, "What have you been up to?"*
> *Satan answered GOD, "Going here and there, checking things out on earth."*
> *GOD said to Satan, "Have you noticed my friend Job? There's no one quite like him—honest and true to his word, totally devoted to God and hating evil."*
> *Satan retorted, "So do you think Job does all that out of the sheer goodness of his heart? Why, no one ever had it so good! You pamper him like a pet, make sure nothing bad ever happens to him or his family or his possessions, bless everything he does—he can't lose!*
> *"But what do you think would happen if you reached down and took away everything that is his? He'd curse you right to your face, that's what."*
> *GOD replied, "We'll see. Go ahead—do what you want with all that is his. Just don't hurt him." Then Satan left the presence of GOD.*
> Job 1:6-12 (MSG)

Permission! Not really the permission we want God to give, but if we consider it this way—nothing is out of the Master's hand. He is with us, loves us and is praying for us in all things. It's like cross-stitch. We always see the front—a beautiful picture with some encouraging words that may even be hanging in a lovely frame. But, if you turn it over, all you see a big tangled mess. Yes, you can tell what colors have been used, if there are pictures or words, but the threads are knotted, tangled, and no image is distinguishable. From our earthly perspective, we only see the back of the cross-stitch. Life can look like a jumbled up mess from our vantage point, but God sees the entire beautiful picture that He's creating in us and through us. In the big tangled mess, His exquisite plan is disguised but rest assured every thread is in place, every word, and picture crystal clear so His work will be displayed and known. May we all find rest in the truth of His word and His promises of protection more than we ever have.

PRAYER

Father, guard our hearts and minds against the lie that when someone or something in our lives isn't perfect, or we are in a holding pattern for answers or solutions, that you have left us. Open our eyes to the lies of the enemy (Satan), remind us to lift our eyes to You, so we are reminded of the truth. The truth that you are always with us, you are for us, you pray for us and love us beyond measure. Father, you didn't promise all pain, suffering, and tears would end until your glorious return. As we wait for that day, even when our lives aren't perfect, happy, and joyful may we find peace, strength, and courage through You and You alone. In your loving name, Amen.

SAMMY

"You buy the house; we'll buy the boat."

Who comes out ahead in that exchange remains to be seen, especially if stories like the bungled boat sale continue to abound.

Our family was ecstatic when "Uncle Dan," my wife's brother, decided to buy a lake house at a mid-point between our home in North Carolina and his in Virginia. He wanted to create a family retreat that would allow us to see each other more. We offered to buy the boat so we could see more of the lake while we saw more of each other.

Unfortunately, we bought the wrong boat.
Wrong motor.
Wrong style for our family.
Wrong, wrong, wrong.

The attempt at a boat ownership do-over in year two of our new summer life at "Butler Cabin" is when I started to feel that it may be easier to write the check for the mortgage than it would be to serve as boat owner and manager.

After shopping around for a new party barge (I mean...pontoon boat) we decided on one at a small boat dealer nearby. Seeing as we had a boat to sell, we weren't in a huge hurry to pull the trigger on buying the new one. We were happy when a happy medium was presented by the boat store owner, "You can just put your old boat on consignment here, and I'll try to sell it for you since you aren't in town all the time. If you can get what you want out of it and I make $500, I'm happy." *I don't have to handle test drives or negotiations or paperwork, did you say? Sign me up!* Great plan, except for the "signing up" part—we didn't sign a thing. Forty-three years on this planet and I didn't think to get an agreement in writing? Shame on me. Sixty-three years on this planet (I'm guessing) and Mr. Boat Dealer didn't get anything in writing either? Double-shame on him! He's the dealer; he should've known the importance a little bit more than me, I figure.

None of this "in writing" stuff was a problem until we found a buyer on our own who stated that he wanted only to deal directly with us. On a Wednesday about a month-and-a-half after we started the consignment attempt, I let Sammy-the-boat-dealer know that I would be there after hours that weekend to pick up the old boat. I told him I was sorry that his efforts to sell it had not been successful and that we were going to give it a go on our own. I also reiterated my appreciation for his great service by selling us a new boat, a purchase we had gone ahead and completed with him less than a week earlier.

Sure, Scott…here's a bill for my services, is essentially what he said next.
As our kids love to say, "Wait…what?"

A bill? For work you did on my old boat? For work you did on my old boat over two weeks ago? For work you did on my old boat over two weeks ago that I never asked you to do nor authorized? A bill for $482.26—an amount perilously close to the $500 you would have made had you sold the boat when it was on consignment? Yeah, ummm, THAT doesn't feel right. THAT feels like sour grapes.

Fortunately, the discussion about this bill didn't take place until the week following our successful sale of the old, wrong, wrong, wrong for us boat.

Unfortunately, the discussion ended with his threat to take me to court.

I soul-searched in a big way over this situation. I'm not the guy to screw the little boat dealer in the small town by not paying a bill he has presented to me. I'm also not the guy to go to court. I don't have the interest or emotional bandwidth for that kind of negativity in my life. However, after having explained my perspective and listening to his, I did what felt right and is often an agreeable solution for situations like this—I offered to split it and pay half of the bill. I hadn't asked him to do the work, but he had improved an asset of mine, and perhaps those improvements had helped with the sale of the boat. He had concerns over putting a boat "on the road" with any issues that he thought were important to fix, seeing as the boat was going to have his business name attached to it. A misunderstanding, much like the one that happened in my neighborhood at the same time I was trying to find the resolve to this agreement that wasn't an agreement because we weren't smart enough to put it in writing.

*

Anger.
That is the emotion I felt when I read a neighbor's post on the neighborhood Facebook page. She had taken a picture of a note that had blown into her yard that said—in thick, red ink—"Not responsible for your pets. I have poison in my yard. Thank you." She was angry. She felt as though her tranquil life had been shattered by a mean neighbor who didn't like animals.

It's one thing to find the note but imagine how you'd feel if you were part of our family, living in the same neighborhood and having just lost a healthy, awesome, fun three-year-old cat to sudden renal failure a few months prior. Our Veterinarian had suggested that poisoning was one of the most likely causes of her death at such a young age.

Anger.

My first comment on the neighborhood page showed my anger, as did my post on my own page. Then I let grace creep in, and my thoughts and comments went to praying for the best for the perpetrator. My prayer was that they would be found out and given some guidance toward channeling such hate and anger toward good, rather than their efforts and energy going to something so negative and hateful.

And then this happened...

A neighbor 'fessed up that this was *her* note. She had posted it on a stake at the edge of her yard **FOR GOOD**—to warn people walking by with their dogs that she had put down a pesticide that was harmful to animals. (Yes, you can take a second to re-read what her note said and, no, we can't argue about pesticides right now.) She posted this note out of *kindness* to animals, *not hate* for them.

Context.

How incredibly different is this note when it's fastened to a stake in someone's yard than it is when it blows off and lands on someone else's? It went from a well-intended warning to what was construed as a nasty threat.

Respond don't react.
Use the right words.
Show grace.
Assume the best.
Forgive.
Err to the positive.

The lessons from this misunderstanding are many. Rather than hoping for the worst for the author of this note, I began praying there would be more people in this world who are like her. What a difference a few minutes can make.

*

I published virtually those same words as a blog post on the Friday morning before Sammy's self-imposed Monday deadline, the deadline he set to proceed with his threat to go to the Magistrate's office to start court proceedings. Then I got in the shower and heard God speak to me. He gave me the perfect answer to the boat repair bill—at least the perfect answer for me, and my conscience, at that moment in time: *Two checks. Send him two checks.*

I proceeded to print out a copy of my blog post about misunderstandings, wrote a handwritten note to Sammy to tell him that I understand that he's not the guy who just does work on people's boats for no reason and without their permission and that I'm not the guy who just doesn't pay his bills and put all of it in an envelope.

I also included two checks, each for half the amount of the bill he had presented to me.

Let him decide.

After reading my blog post, reading my note and perhaps reading a little about me online, maybe he'll decide he was wrong and tear them up. Or maybe he'll take the gentlemen's agreement I had offered and meet in the middle by cashing just one of them. Who knows, perhaps he's steadfast in his belief that he did no wrong and felt fully entitled to the whole amount, even after considering that I had just stroked him a check for over $20,000 for a new boat and could be a repeat service customer and referral source for years to come.

Either way, I'm good.

I know I put my best foot forward and tried to do the right thing. I know I avoided the negativity involved with a court battle (which an attorney and many others said I would have won easily). I know that I did all I could to preserve a relationship that I may need to lean on in the future.

Paul Harvey was famous for telling us "The rest of the story." In this case, it's that Sammy cashed both checks the day he got them, I've had to call his mechanic twice about issues with the new boat, and half my friends think I'm brilliant for sending two checks while the other half think I'm nuts for paying him even a nickel. Personally, I'm just happy to know that I listened to God when He spoke to me. Now, if I could listen when He tells me **through everyone I know who has ever owned a boat** that I should never buy a boat! "The two best days..."—you've heard that line about owning a boat as many times as I have, I'm sure.

Mess to message: *Thank you, Sammy. You helped me learn a life lesson about perspective and listening to the Lord when He speaks to me. You weren't just a stubborn man trying to keep a business afloat but one full of integrity and steadfast belief in his work.*

† TAKING THE LOW ROAD †

Would Scott's lessons have been as impactful if he had let anger rule his actions? What are some of the things we can put into practice in our own lives that make us slow to anger and look at things from another's perspective? How do we turn it all over to God, as Scott did, listen and sit in gratitude and satisfaction when people don't do the right thing? I wonder if Sammy will ever find God and allow Him to change his heart? Or as one friend said, "I wonder if Sammy knows God, followed what he believes God told him to do, and sleeps peacefully feeling he did the right thing?"

I have a super organized Type A personality. Some think that's a great thing, but like most things, it has its pros and cons. Yes, my sink is usually dish free, but my heart can struggle without a clear list from God about how to live the life He has called me to. Let me say, I'm grateful He didn't give us a list and I understand why He didn't. We would become just like the Pharisees in the Bible who grew cold and condemning from following laws and crossing things off a list to secure their relationship with God instead of seeking Him on a personal level. They didn't realize how self-defeating, legalistic and insincere just following the rules was when it came to being a Christ follower.

That said, the scriptures can be daunting, but I have a strong desire to live my life in a way that honors and looks more like Christ. So imagine how awesome it was for this Type A girl to find in 1 Thessalonians a set of 22 commandments (laws, edicts, orders, precepts, or rules—whatever you want to call it) for Christians from the apostle Paul.

Not commandments from God's mouth like the Ten Commandments found in Exodus 20 (because if you are a Christian, these can be easy to skim over) but something more descript. I remember the mindset I had in my prayers as an ill-equipped young Christian. At night when I was supposed to confess my sins, I would think to myself, "I didn't cuss, kill, steal or commit adultery, so I think I'm ok in the sin department." How wrong! How terribly wrong!

I adore how Paul takes it one step further in 1 Thessalonians, giving some clear and intentional instructions on what it should look like after we say, "God, I believe in your son, Jesus. I believe He came, walked this earth, died, was buried and rose again. I understand and thank you for the fact that He suffered and died for me on that cross. He has covered all my sins." Seriously, how do we live after accepting a gift like that? Scott undoubtedly shows us one example in his story about Sammy, but what else can we do?

Paul shares excellent insight in his letter to the Thessalonians. I used the ESV translation and added in numbers in parentheses for each of Paul's commandments so you wouldn't miss them. (Please note the numbers are not the verse numbers, but how I numbered the lessons.)

Therefore (1) encourage one another and (2) build one another up, just as you are doing. We ask you, brothers, to (3) respect those who labor among you and are over you in the Lord and admonish you, and (4) to esteem them very highly in love because of their work. (5) Be at peace among yourselves. And we urge you, brothers, (6) admonish the idle, (7) encourage the fainthearted, (8) help the weak, (9) be patient with them all. (10) See that no one repays anyone evil for evil, but (11) always seek to do good to one another and to everyone. (12) Rejoice always, (13) pray without ceasing, (14) give thanks in all circumstances; for this is the will of God in Christ Jesus for you. (15) Do not quench the Spirit. (16) Do not despise prophecies, (17) but test everything; (18) hold fast what is good. (19) Abstain from every form of evil. Now may the God of peace himself sanctify you completely, and may your whole spirit and soul and body be kept blameless at the coming of our Lord Jesus Christ. He who calls you is faithful; he will surely do it. Brothers, (20) pray for us. (21) Greet all the brothers with a holy kiss. I put you under oath before the Lord to (22) have this letter read to all the brothers. 1 Thessalonians 5:11-25

Are you speechless? It may not be your first time reading these verses, but maybe like me, they fell fresh on your heart. Something struck me as I looked at the verses running together with loving, direct and clear instructions from Paul. It's a list! A beautiful list and it's an answer to prayer for me and all of us. Clear instructions on how to live like we believe Christ died for us. I pray you are as inspired by these verses as I am.

When we can keep these goals in mind, as I think Scott did in his boat fiasco, I believe it will help each of us put into practice the gifts of grace, forgiveness, and love Jesus taught so that we can learn the heart treasures/lessons that God desires to show us. We can only control our actions, not the actions of others, and must be confident leaving the rest to God. When we allow God into every situation we face, it can be effortless to take the "high road." Or is it the "low road?" Consider this. Choosing the high road actually boils down to taking the low road. I know that sounds a little counter-intuitive and like I've been out in the sun too long, but stick with me. When we take the low road, we are essentially putting ourselves last; putting others before ourselves and loving others as we love ourselves. Dying to self, putting pride aside, taking the lowest place ensures we handle life and its' situations with integrity and grace, but this can only be done when we position ourselves below others, hence, taking the low road.

We aren't able to take the high road if we are living on it. I picture my son sitting on our back patio; feet kicked up on the coffee table, and drinking a lemonade saying, "Oh, yeah! I'm living the high life." When our lives, actions, prayers, and faith are all about us and our comfort, we are living a life literally "high on SELF." When we lower our posture to one of servanthood and humility, as Jesus did, we see the benefits of the low road.

I am the Vine; you are the branches. When you're joined with me and I with you, the relation intimate and organic, the harvest is sure to be abundant. Separated, you can't produce a thing. Anyone who separates from me is deadwood, gathered up and thrown on the bonfire. But if you make yourselves at home with me and my words are at home in you, you can be sure that whatever you ask will be listened to and acted upon. This is how my Father shows who he is—when you produce grapes, when you mature as my disciples. John 15:5-8 (MSG)

We can't take the low road or follow the twenty-two qualities we find in 1 Thessalonians without God's power, courage and strength. 1 Thessalonians 5:19 says, *"Do not quench the Spirit."* If we do not follow this precept, we will never bare the fruit God desires in our life. Even though Sammy didn't take the low road, Scott hasn't allowed Sammy's negative actions to quench the Spirit in his life. Pause here for a moment and ponder these five words:

Do not quench the Spirit!

I've pondered their meaning for hours, and many thoughts have rolled through my head. If we define quench and Spirit and reread these five words, it does so much to deepen our understanding. Let me throw out a few variations for you:

Do not extinguish the Fountain of Life (Psalm 36:9, 87:7)
Do not suppress the Consuming Fire (Deut. 4:24)
Do not extinguish the Thirst Quencher (John 4:13-14)
Do not suppress the Spring of Living Water (Jer 2:13)

These concepts work against human nature because when we have climbed to the tip-top of a mountain (with a REALLY hefty backpack) to enjoy the view, we are thirsty and drink all we can to quench that thirst we have built up.

Human nature also beckons us to race into action when there is a fire consuming lives, homes and beautiful forests. The desire to extinguish the damaging and deadly fire is so natural within us; we often act without thinking things through. However, when it comes to the Living God, the Holy Spirit who dwells in us, we need to work with the opposite frame of mind; working against human nature and the world. Paul reminds us (1 Thessalonians) that we are never to satisfy, extinguish, suppress or quench the Holy Spirit. In other words, we need to look beyond ourselves, our plans, our perceived strengths and rely on that of the Holy Spirit. If I had written this commandment/guideline, I would have said, "Quench Yourself, Not the Spirit!" We never want to rid ourselves of the desire to seek our Heavenly Father and follow the plans He has for us. We never want to extinguish the passion we have to find Him daily and in all things.

PRAYER

Heavenly Father, I pray you will give us an unquenchable thirst for Your Word, Your ways, and Your plans. As we sit and fill up on Your written Word, consume our hearts with the desire to follow Your ways and laws above all else. Extinguish our worldly desires, barriers to hearing Your whisper and sinful ways and thoughts. May we seek you daily without hesitation for every task and situation we face and hear Your answer above all the other noise around and within us. In Your Mighty name, we pray, Amen.

LISA & TIM

Selflessness. When I hear that word, I think of the military and first responders and moms. I also think of Lisa at the Apple® Store.

I will never forget the smell of the scented candle in my mother's nursing home room during her last hours. I will never forget the sound of the wooden flute that was played by the Hospice volunteer. I will never forget the acts of kindness from my family, the staff and my dear friend, Bobby. For some reason, though, I thought I *would* *not* remember the look of the room and my mother's face, so I took some pictures on my iPhone. Creepy for some to read that, I know, yet understood entirely by others.

After a phone call from the nurse at 5 a.m. to tell me that my mom's breathing and skin had started to show changes, I made the twenty-minute drive to Rex Rehabilitation and Nursing Care in Raleigh and spent the next twenty-eight hours awake at my mom's bedside. During that time, I ate and drank from the fully-stocked cart that the staff had waiting for me upon my arrival, shared some stories with my wife and her mom and watched the national championship on TV with Bobby.

Shortly after Bobby arrived, fairly fresh off his own end-of-life experience with his father, he and I agreed that the light coming from the long, fluorescent light on the wall above my mom's head was offensive to us and likely to her as well, even though her eyes never opened that day. We looked around for a solution and found her dark purple hair-cutting cape from the salon hanging behind her door. We draped this over the wooden valance that ran in front of the long bulb. The fire hazard it created proved to be worth it as it was just what the room needed; it created a soft, purple tone to the room that was soothing and comfortable for all who entered. I was alone with my mom in that calming environment from the time Bobby left (around 11 p.m.) until she took her last breath a few hours later. It was during that window of time that I felt compelled to capture the environment in a few pictures.

Those pictures, along with other "last pictures" of my mom in some happier times, were in peril when—on a Saturday morning a couple of weeks after her passing—I turned on my phone and got nothing but the dreaded "Connect to iTunes" screen. After trying out tips from Google searches and help forums, I found myself headed to the Apple® Store.

As I walked into the crowded store, I was greeted by my newest friend Lisa; a twenty-something-year-old girl with welcoming, kind green eyes. Little did Lisa know when she headed to work that day that those kind eyes would shed a few tears before she returned home. In as composed of a manner as I could muster, I told Lisa the story of my mom, the pictures and the phone. Her sincere interest in helping was clear and then made more and more clear as we went through a series of fix-it attempts.

She thought of things we could try. We tried. No luck.

She went to a co-worker to get ideas. We tried. No luck.

She went to the "Genius" desk to see what they could come up with. We tried. No luck.

Lisa's last-ditch effort was to call the Jedi Master of the iPhone at home as he was off-duty that morning. This time she came back to me with nothing to try and with two bloodshot, misty red eyes as well; Lisa had been crying in the back room after being told there was nothing else they could do. Call it hyperbole, but the parallel that this drew for me to a family member being told by a doctor that there was nothing further they could do for the patient was tangible and obvious at that moment.

Lisa works at the Apple® Store, with electronics. She knows, however, that what she does and for whom she does it is so much more than that—Lisa is a person who works with people. In the sea of humanity that was in the store that Saturday morning, I was floored to find a kind-hearted person who just *gets it*. She walked away countless times, but she never left me. This was obvious when she came back to me—after we had hugged it out a couple of times—to hand me a new, free phone. That phone was a consolation gift that meant the world to me not due to the saved cost, but due to the compassion behind it. Lisa's manager had given the "ok" for her to do this and, when I asked for the manager to come speak to me so I could thank him, it was obvious he had been moved to tears as well. His manager (Lisa's boss's boss) was also in the store that day, and *he too* had sweaty eyeballs when he spoke to me on my way out the door. Tears and hugs at the Apple® Store. It all started with those kind eyes that belong to my forever friend, Lisa.

*

Lisa did what author Tim Sanders teaches, and she doesn't even know it. She showed "bizlove."

In the early years of my marriage and career, all I read was the newspaper. I likened reading a book—especially a business book— to getting an injection with a big, thick needle. Was. Not. Interested. I had worked for a company for seven years that did next-to-nothing to help its employees with self-improvement and personal growth; a very "me first" environment. My thoughts erred toward,

I don't want to associate with him; he's the competition.
I don't want to share my idea with her; she'll steal it.

I'm not going to tell him the trick; he might get credit for it.

After changing employers to one that encouraged self-improvement, I hired a business and life coach. Shortly after that, I found myself at a conference in Palm Springs where a sharp-dressed, skinny tie-wearin', techy-lookin' dude from LA named Tim Sanders gave the keynote. I dismissed him. Then I fell in love with him. Like man-crush, I love his mojo, I-want-to-**be**-him-one-day in love with him. The dude just gets it like Lisa just gets it. [He also returns emails and is willing to stay in touch with e-stalkers from his audience, so I hear.]

I'll never forget the activity he led us through to illustrate one of the fundamental truths behind his message. It involved loose change, which people actually had in their pockets in 2005. Tim had us stand up—all 2,000 of us—dig into our pockets and grab our loose change in our fists. Then he asked us to close our eyes and hold our hands out in front of us. "Now drop it," he said. After the clanging of the coins on the ballroom floor ceased, Tim said, "Congratulations, you just donated to the hurricane victims in Florida." (We later found out that the total was over $3,000—what a cool activity!)

Tim's message was this—we all suffer from scarcity thinking. As we held that money in our fists, our minds were going through a laundry list of reasons why we hoped he wouldn't ask us to part with it. Too many of us live our lives like this.

Thankfully, I walked out of that conference with a copy of Tim's book, *Love is the Killer App*, and a whole new attitude based on bringing love into business—'BIZLOVE' as he calls it. My generosity and kindness toward others in business (and outside of business as well because you can't help but change both) skyrocketed and became the director of my thoughts, words, and actions. I learned to "use reckless generosity" in life as another author, Scott Ginsberg likes to say.

Don't just tell her about a book, send her a copy.

Don't just tell him there's a great guy who does <u>X</u> that he should meet, introduce them.

Don't just say, "I'm sorry for your loss" when a colleague's father passes away, go to the funeral.

I was so attracted to this message of love yet, at the time, had not yet received the invitation from Allen that you read about earlier; Tim's talk was a couple of years before that gift was given to me. In hindsight, I believe the introduction to Tim and his message was God grabbing hold of me by the lower leg, picking up my foot and placing it on the first stepping-stone of my faith journey. I was so enamored with Tim's approach to life (the Christian life, just not called that in his speeches), yet his invitation did not happen at a church but in a business setting instead; sneaky Jesus in action. He cracked the door a little before He opened it fully for me years later.

I have lived the "Lovecat" approach to life, as Tim Sanders calls it, since 2005 and will attest that sharing your knowledge, your network and your compassion goes further than you could ever imagine. In some cases, showing up in life with love as your lead will even birth a chapter in a book about you.

Mess to message: *Thank you, Lisa and Tim. Put simply; you live lives worth imitating. Both of you helped me in immeasurable ways by showing me love in action. The multiplier effect of your focus on love will show itself in ways you may never know, but now you know how it helped me.*

† AN IRRIGATED GARDEN †

Lisa took extraordinary measures to help Scott in the middle of a hectic workday. How did she have the heart to press pause on the world around her and know the time she spent with Scott was more critical that particular day? We don't get to hear Tim's "before" story; we only see the amazing blessings he has produced and shared with others to make their workplaces better. What drives him to focus on love above all else? Were they ever afraid of the repercussions they might face if they were more heart-centered in the workplace?

They will come and shout for joy on the heights of Zion; they will be radiant with joy because of the LORD's goodness, because of the grain, the new wine, the fresh oil, and because of the young of the flocks and herds. Their life will be like an irrigated garden, and they will no longer grow weak from hunger. Jeremiah 31:12 (HCSB)

I know you are wondering where gardening comes into this story, but as I considered both Lisa and Tim's story I couldn't help but wonder how they got above the noise, numbers, and quotas to share love and kindness. That led me to these verses in Jeremiah. I couldn't stop myself from reading these words over and over again: **"Their life will be like an irrigated garden."** What a beautiful image of what our life can look like with God in it. I believe both Lisa and Tim have irrigated gardens/hearts.

My mom has a green thumb, while mine is more of a brown thumb so instead of trusting my instincts I looked into the benefits of irrigation. It's incredible how much they relate to all the benefits and blessings we can experience when we allow God into our hearts. For example:

1. Irrigation is vital because crops can't depend only on the rain.
Like crops, we should not depend on only ourselves if we are going to be successful in patience, forgiveness, grace, courage, faith, etc. Relying solely on ourselves will lead to failure, disappointment and no harvest.

2. Irrigation allows one to produce a greater volume of crops. Like irrigation, God can equip and lead us to yield an abundance of fruit, the fruit of the Spirit.

But the fruit of the Spirit is love, joy, peace, patience, kindness, goodness, faithfulness, gentleness, self-control; against such things there is no law. Galatians 5:22-23 (ESV)

3. With irrigated fields, the outcome is more stable and reliable. You can be more confident that your growing goals will be met.

With God, who is the same today as He was yesterday and will always be, we can count on a consistent strength and supply of grace, love, and forgiveness. We can trust that when He calls us, no matter what He calls us to do, He will equip us with all we need to complete the task.

4. Irrigation allows for continuous cultivation.

Following God daily and gleaning the truth from His word gives us a growing and deepening understanding of His heart, ways, and desires. It also allows us to follow Him closely in our daily lives and not stray from His path, so we have a heart that looks more like His every day.

5. Finally, irrigation reduces the fluctuations and the risk of crop failure due to drought.

With God in the center of our lives and our eyes looking to the cross, we are less likely to have fluctuations in our hearts and minds. We are less likely to succumb to sinful and selfish desires when we are living close to God and in His word. Please notice I said we are "less likely," not guaranteed. We will falter and fall many times, but with God's grace we can pick ourselves up, dust off and try again.

Overall, there are so many more benefits to living, loving, believing, and following our faithful Father in Heaven. I don't know about you, but I want my life to be like an irrigated garden that never grows weak or weary, that produces fruit pleasing to our Father and sustains me through the splendor and the desert. I believe Lisa and Tim have shown us that they do too.

But sometimes, fear can get in the way of us cultivating an irrigated garden. Jeremiah has something to say about that too.

Let's set the stage: The Lord calls upon Jeremiah to go and speak without fear about all He has shared with him. Of course, Jeremiah, like many before him, says, *"Oh no, Lord, GOD! Look, I don't know how to speak since I am only a youth."* (Jeremiah 1:6, HCSB) and then the Lord reached out His hand to touch Jeremiah's mouth and says, *"I have now filled your mouth with My words."* (v. 9)

The image of God reaching out to touch Jeremiah's mouth makes my heart leap. Like Lisa and Tim, have you ever been in one of those situations where you have been able to speak a gentle truth, offer a comforting word or submissively follow in a way that wasn't your own? In a way that you know you never would have never been able to do if God hadn't stretched out His hand and filled your mouth with His words and your heart with His love? God did this for me when I ran into a friend's husband who had recently left her and their children for another woman. My flesh would have preferred to punch him in the gut and then call him a few names while he was down. But with the Holy Spirit, I was able to graciously inquire about his work and children with a prayerful heart. I knew that encounter was all under God's control. It's an incredible feeling. I'm so thankful God is able to work in my heart and keep "me, myself, and I" from getting in the way of His plan if I allow Him in.

My personal prayer that I offer up daily is, "Not me, but You God!" There is a reason for that. When our hearts are full of God's Word and love, and fully irrigated, we can more easily step back and allow God to do His work through us.

And the marvelous promises from Jeremiah's story don't end there. God gives Jeremiah two visions. The first one is this:

Then the word of the LORD came to me, asking, "What do you see, Jeremiah?" I replied, "I see a branch of an almond tree." The LORD said to me, "You have seen correctly, for I watch over My word to accomplish it." Again the word of the LORD came to me inquiring, "What do you see?" Jeremiah 1:11-13 (HCSB)

Here is what God lit up in lights for me to see—*"...for I watch over My word to accomplish it."*

This is the kind of revelation and reminder that keeps me coming back, day after day, to God's word. We often envision God looking down from Heaven and watching over us, but have you ever considered that He watches over His word so that it's accomplished? To picture Him watching over His word is such an incredible image and a great reminder. God is close! He is in every teeny tiny detail, He sees all, knows all and will accomplish all He has promised and declared.

Those nine words make my arms lift up in joy, my eyes look to the heavens, my heart leap with gladness and my spirit soar with faith and hope. When Scott's world seemed to be falling apart, Lisa was there, and then Tim raised him to a new level and showed him how to love in the workplace. Not only did they have hearts that were prepared for God to use them but, because their gardens were irrigated, they understood how critical it was to press pause on life and make time to share love with others.

Knowing when to press pause can be a tall order in this world of instant communication, instant grits, instant popcorn, and instant gratification. You name it, and we can access it any minute of the day. Will you join me in trying to press the pause button when it comes to our lives and making room to share the kindness and love of Christ?

PRAYER

Heavenly Father, you are an awesome God! I pray we honor You in all ways, praise You for your power, and embrace You with all our heart so we can serve You with every cell. You are here with us and in control. Help us to cling to that truth so that all fear and uncertainty we have will be cast off to make room for you to come in and irrigate our hearts. Use us for Your purpose, will and plan as we trust Your way is perfect even when we don't understand. Please give us the strength and courage to attain this goal and keep our eyes on You as we strive to live lives worthy of the Gospel. In Your name, we pray, Amen.

JANINE AND MICHAEL

I could hear the heavy equipment as I typed from the comfort of my living room. This is how close our family lived to St. Mary Magdalene Catholic Church which, since its' founding, had met in the gymnasium of the school that shares its name. It wouldn't be long before a beautiful new church building sat beside the school, a project so many had quietly yet eagerly awaited as they sat in plastic chairs rather than beautiful wooden pews. One of the most devoted daughters of the church was in her glory when it was complete.

Janine stands about 5-foot nothin'—one of the many ways, I believe, she resembles Mother Teresa. Such a comparison may sound like exaggeration and is certainly one Janine would scoff at, but her work is essential, and she is incredibly good at it. Janine runs the middle and high school youth ministry program along with her fellow rock star, Liz. My wife and I were blessed to find out about this program just as our daughter was reaching the age at which she could participate.

The gym is where "The EDGE" meets on Sunday evenings. The chairs used for Mass are cleared away, and a very cool environment is created by a team of volunteers. A series of white curtains and modern lamps are placed in a way that allows the teens to feel like they are in a cozy place, not a cavernous gymnasium. With the backdrop of a screen fed by a projector and a crucifix that stands six feet high, Janine corrals, rallies and educates over 250 middle-schoolers. She does so in their language and at their speed, with the Gospel at the center. Her large-group teaching will typically include a funny skit, video or story: sometimes all three. Our time together is short, with the large group session usually lasting 10-20 minutes, followed by a small-group time where leaders like me will take ten or so kids to a quiet area of the school to break apart the message of the night.

On a chilly night in March, after discussing the subject deeply with her family, Janine shared a very personal story with the group. It was apparent from her tone that this was serious, private, and not to be shared outside the group. She is the mother of three boys and the wife of a strong, resilient Marine. For her to share a challenge that faced one of her boys—a participant in The EDGE who was in the room that night—could not have been easy. Fortunately, she is very good at listening to God's voice and was able to connect the dots, months later, from an experience she had with a young lady in the program who was living through the same challenges as her son. She said, "I knew what to do because of what was given to us." She made her mess into her message.

The inherent message of Janine's story was on the topic of unanswered prayers and the story she told demonstrated the value that unanswered prayers can hold; the value is they are not unanswered, just that they may *seem* so. The challenge that Janine's family had been living through had seemingly been fraught with one unanswered prayer after another. Yet her story, told in a setting more quiet than the quietest church, taught a life lesson that I believe will never be forgotten by the silent teenagers who listened that night. I know this because of what happened just after our group went from 200 to 10, from large group to small.

As we folded up our blanket and walked to our quiet spot in a carpeted stairwell just off the gym, it was apparent that the five boys and five girls were in a different place emotionally than they had been when they walked in that evening. Quiet. They had heard— *really heard*—the story and these teenagers were quiet. The two high school kids who assisted our group were without words as well. Once settled in our familiar spot, we started to break into bite-sized pieces what we had just taken in. Having done a lot of public speaking in my life, I couldn't help but point out that the most effective speeches are typically those that include stories. Janine had just taken something incredibly personal and told a story—and she owned the room. A conversation ensued about how a number of the kids in our small group had personal experience with the same kind of challenge Janine had spoken about. This commonality was welcomed as it added even more to the power of the night.

I sat on the landing just inside the door and faced up the stairs where two of the girls and three of the boys sat. Three other girls sat to my right with the high school helpers beside them. To my left—between the steps and me—sat Michael who proceeded to create a memory our small group will never forget.

As we started to talk about unanswered prayers, I posed a question, "Have any of you had an experience with unanswered prayers, maybe even where something not-so-good turned into something good?" This was a tall order for seventh graders, so I fully expected to hear crickets. Instead, I got the ultimate blessing for a small-group leader, a quick 'yes.' From my left, Michael answered, "Yes, I do." He continued, "My father lost his job about six months ago. We prayed and prayed for a new job to come quickly, but it didn't. Because of this, he had a lot of time on his hands, so he went up to New York to visit my grandparents…" His voice immediately cracked, and this seventh-grade boy started bawling. He was crying uncontrollably, almost unable to catch his breath. Just as Janine had absolute quiet during her story, Michael received the same gift from his peers and this leader. After what seemed like ten minutes but was probably just one, I inched my way over and tried to calm him. I put my hand on his shoulder and suggested some deep breaths. He took a few, and they helped some, but not enough to get him fully back. The room remained quiet as I offered him an out, "Do you want to step out and collect yourself?" Michael shook his head 'no.' His steel amazed me.

After another minute or so, this brave boy finished his story. "While my dad was up there, my grandfather died unexpectedly. If my father's prayers had been answered and he had gotten another job right away, he wouldn't have been there when it happened." The awe of this moment was palpable. I fully believe that every kid in that stairwell got it. They learned one of the most valuable lessons they may ever learn—that God doesn't ignore your prayers, He answers them in ways that fit His perfect plan—in ways that serve the greater good. They got it.

Before every EDGE meeting, the leaders met in the small chapel on the second floor of the gymnasium building. My prayer was always the same—that God would give Janine and the small-group leaders the words that the kids needed to hear. On this night, *my* prayer went unanswered—I had no words after the story from that brave little boy. Actually, maybe it *was* answered, it's just that He used brave Michael's words instead of mine.

Mess to message: *A story shared by an adult opens up the door for a normally shy and quiet seventh-grade boy to share a story close to his heart. Thank you, Janine, for listening to what is obviously your calling and thank you, Michael, for following her lead and making yourself vulnerable for the benefit of others.*

† BUT WHY? †

How had Janine grown her faith so much that she was able to place fear and judgment aside to share her personal story? Had Michael's parents sat down and shared with him how incredible God had been or had he already grown enough in his faith to notice it himself? I wonder how this young man's faith grew after seeing God at work in his family's circumstances and how many times he will share the story throughout his lifetime?

As I look back and reflect on my early thirties, it's a blur of deep emotion. In the course of a year, I had a friend who died from cancer, my Dad went through prostate cancer, my daughter had a scary medical ordeal, and one of her friends (Ella, who you read about in chapter 2) was diagnosed with a terminal tumor on her brain stem. It was a heart heavy and distressing time. They say God counts each tear that falls. Let's just say, He was super busy with me during that time. I'm sure Janine and Michael felt the same.

My friends and I would sit, pray and discuss all we were enduring and wonder what in the world God was doing. Looking back, it's clear that no mistake had been made when He had woven this group of women together. God knew we would need one another. He didn't create us to be alone. For us, it seemed to be one battle and heartache after another, never giving any of us a chance to catch our breath.

There were many unanswered prayers during that time. Marriages ended when betrayals continued, children had cancer treatments (some survived, and some didn't), and friends with children who were in our praying circle didn't make it to see their children get out of elementary school and continue to thrive. But God never left my side and gave me strength and courage in those situations.

He comforts us in all our affliction, so that we may be able to comfort those who are in any kind of affliction, through the comfort we ourselves receive from God. For as the sufferings of Christ overflow to us, so through Christ our comfort also overflows. 2 Corinthians 1:4-5 (HCSB)

However, as it's expressed in Philippians 1:12, really sums it up:

Now I want you to know, brothers, that what has happened to me has actually resulted in the advance of the gospel. (HCSB)

This verse from Philippians is about Paul. He was beaten by the crowds, but able to share his testimony with them, so he saw it as an opportunity and not a devastation (Acts 21-26). After being beaten, he was transported from noble leaders to kings and then from prison to dangerous sea transfers. All along the way, having the opportunity to bend the ear of many audiences including King Agrippa, Festus, Caesar, Ananias, Felix, and even jailors, prison mates, and sailors. Paul saw his trials as a blessing and took advantage of these audiences to share his great testimony and advance the gospel.

After all, Paul had quite the testimony. He had been a hater and persecutor of Christians and God until he had an encounter with Him [God] personally on the Road to Damascus. I hope you will read the story in its entirety in Acts 9, but here is a little taste.

Now as he went on his way, he approached Damascus, and suddenly a light from heaven shone around him. And falling to the ground, he heard a voice saying to him, "Saul, Saul, why are you persecuting me?" And he said, "Who are you, Lord?" And he said, "I am Jesus, whom you are persecuting. But rise and enter the city, and you will be told what you are to do." The men who were traveling with him stood speechless, hearing the voice but seeing no one. Saul rose from the ground, and although his eyes were opened, he saw nothing. So they led him by the hand and brought him into Damascus. And for three days he was without sight, and neither ate nor drank. Acts 9:3-9 (ESV)

Fast-forward more than ten years, and I can see that the affliction my friends and I endured offered God the opportunity to provide comfort, strength, and courage for us all in miraculous ways. Please notice that I didn't say, fast-forward ten minutes, two weeks or even ten months. It took me years to begin to see the benefit and fruit that could come from the pain. In my ministry and life, I can understand and sympathize with others in ways I would have never been able to without enduring my own trials. Words that flowed from my heart on to paper for Bible studies would never have been written without those experiences. Without the unanswered prayers for healing from cancer, restored marriages and freedom from addictions I can honestly say I wouldn't be the same person or as effective in ministry. The comfort I received from Christ I can now offer to others as it overflowed from Heaven onto me, I can pour it onto those who cross my path and need compassion and comfort just as Janine, Michael and all of us who have overcome can do as well.

We are pressured in every way but not crushed; we are perplexed but not in despair; we are persecuted but not abandoned; we are struck down but not destroyed. 2 Corinthians 4:8-9 (HCSB)

A lot was lost during that year of my life, and much gained. I was pressed in on every side and clung to God for preservation. Every prayer was not answered, and for a time, it stung and left deep wounds in my heart. I felt slapped to the ground time after time with devastating news and just when I began to regain my strength was knocked down again, but God never forgot me. With His strength and courage, I will never let the suffering I endured or the sadness that can still overcome me, go to waste. He filled those wounds with His great comfort and peace. I will never be the same, but I have committed to using it for His glory and for those He places in my path that need comfort, support, and courage. Thank goodness Janine knows these same truths. We will all suffer in this world, but surely Paul sets a great example for us all because he never faltered in his desire to share the good news and love of Christ in the midst of all he endured.

Faith, even as small as a mustard seed, is all we need sometimes. (Matthew 17:20)

Recently, a friend of mine shared a conversation he had with another friend concerning the unhappiness he felt in his life. My friend told him, "The problem is that you have put God in a box. You have decided who God is without considering who the Bible says He is. You are so busy telling God what you want that you aren't trusting God and allowing Him to work."

One of the ways I try to combat feelings of doubt, fear, worry and not being heard by God is the prayer wall in my pantry. One side is covered with post-it notes full of prayer requests and the other side with praises. It's a fantastic feeling to be able to move a prayer request to the praise side of the wall, but there is something even more powerful. Sometimes when I'm in my closet praying, and my eyes roll across a prayer requests that have been up there for such a long time the post-it note is looking worn and tattered, my heart will begin to ask, "Why God? We have been praying so long for this. Where are you at work in this situation? Why haven't you come through for them yet?" This is where the power of the praise side of the wall comes in, and God whispers to my heart, "Allison, I'm still here. I'm working. In my own time, but I'm in every detail of this mess. Look at all the prayer requests that have become praises as a reminder of that." After His gentle reminder, my eyes scan all the sticky notes that were once requests but now praises. Physical healing, redemption, marital reconciliation, passed exams, safe travels, and the list goes on and on. As I type, tears of gratitude and awe well up in my eyes as I consider all God has done for me and those for whom I pray. The problem is, unless we have a prayer wall or journal where we document it all, the praises can be quickly forgotten and overtaken by the one or two that haven't been answered. When our eyes and heart are more focused on what hasn't happened instead of all the blessings that have been given; doubt, anger, fear, resentment, and anxiety creep in.

Our Father in Heaven knew we would struggle with faith and trust in His ways and wonders. He knew, and Jesus experienced, the temptation of sin we would face while we walk in this flesh. He made sure we had the most effective, loving and complete story of His ways, love, and laws. A "life's little instruction book" to refer to and live by. The trick is that we must open this book—The Bible. We must open it with "eagerness and examine the scriptures" (Acts 17:11) as the early believers did. After all, it tells us many things about our spectacular God!

Our God who made the world and everything in it—He is Lord of heaven and earth and does not live in shrines made by hands. Acts 17:24 (HCSB)

We serve a God who doesn't require everything of us and who loves us because we believe in His Son Jesus Christ and His sacrifice. If we are honest, we will recognize that we don't even deserve the prayers that have been answered. I'm so thankful that's not how God works. Nothing we can do will make Him love us more because He already adores us more than we can fathom. We each have a role to play in His kingdom, gifts He has given us, testimonies to share and people He places in our lives with whom we can share Christ, but He gives the growth. He gives the gifts. He gives the opportunities. He is sovereign and is the ultimate cure giver. If we allow Him to work within us, He will make a way and provide the opportunities to share His message and manage His mysteries. He will give the growth every time we share our story of how He has worked in our lives.

A person should consider us in this way: as servants of Christ and managers of God's mysteries. 1 Corinthians 4:1 (HCSB)

After all, faith has done and accomplished much for the Kingdom of God. Not only that, all the people who made it happen were just like you and me. They were made of flesh, subject to temptation and fell to sin, but with faith they overcame. They were living examples of what we can accomplish with that same faith, they showed us what it looks like and how God honors it. You may have read most of these stories in the Bible, but when you see it listed all in one place (even though what follows here is just a sample), it's breathtaking.

Now faith is the reality of what is hoped for, the proof of what is not seen.

By faith we understand that the universe was created by God's command, so that what is seen has been made from things that are not visible.

By faith Abel offered to God a better sacrifice than Cain did.

By faith Enoch was taken away so he did not experience death, and he was not to be found because God took him away. For prior to his removal he was approved, since he had pleased God.

By faith Noah, after he was warned about what was not yet seen and motivated by godly fear, built an ark to deliver his family.

By faith Abraham, when he was called, obeyed and went out to a place he was going to receive as an inheritance. He went out, not knowing where he was going.

By faith even Sarah herself, when she was unable to have children, received power to conceive offspring, even though she was past the age, since she considered that the One who had promised was faithful.

By faith Abraham, when he was tested, offered up Isaac.

By faith Isaac blessed Jacob and Esau concerning things to come. [21] By faith Jacob, when he was dying, blessed each of the sons of Joseph, and he worshiped, leaning on the top of his staff. [22] By faith Joseph, as he was nearing the end of his life, mentioned the exodus of the Israelites and gave instructions concerning his bones.

By faith, after Moses was born, he was hidden by his parents for three months, because they saw that the child was beautiful, and they didn't fear the king's edict.

By faith the walls of Jericho fell down after being encircled by the Israelites for seven days.

By faith Rahab the prostitute received the spies in peace and didn't perish with those who disobeyed. Hebrews 11:1-31 (NIV)

But what about your life? Have you considered all the ways you have acted "by faith" just as Janine and Michael did in the chapter you just read?

I pray you will join me now and take some time to think about all the times in your life where you acted "by faith" and write out the ways God responded. I can't imagine all the things I've forgotten or overlooked. May God remind us of the fruit of our faith and that we can continue to add to this list all the days of our lives.

PRAYER

Heavenly Father, today we pray for those around us who are still searching, still trying to find the courage to be loved by the Creator, still doubting and still searching for faith. We pray their hearts soften, and they turn their lives over to You. We pray for those who are still relying on their own strength, courage, and wisdom to conquer their sins, trials, and heartbreak. We have no doubt they are tired and weary. Father, open their eyes so they will understand that You want us to come to You weary, broken and sinful. All you ask for is a belief in Your Son Jesus. Father, remind us that despite our circumstances and level of faith, we are loved, cherished and treasured by the Creator of the Universe sink into all our hearts. Please use those of us who believe in and rely on You to shine a light on the path for others that lead them straight to You, our Mighty Savior. Amen.

OWEN

O ne sermon series at 519 Church where Owen preaches and teaches, and I attend and mend, had been about Baptism, entitled "Something in the Water." A week earlier, after having completed my duties on the setup team, I was listening to the band as they rehearsed before worship. Owen is required to be a masterful delegator out of necessity since church met in a CafeGymnaTorium in an elementary school and, therefore, was set up and torn down every week. Holding true to his master delegator self, Owen asked me if I'd do a little project for him, then handed me a full-length mirror and a bag of dirt and asked me to make mud. *This is sooo 519 Church*, I thought to myself—we are creative and edgy as we learn to love well and live differently from our young Pastor who is not fearful of trying new things to make a sermon more memorable. My servant heart and I proceeded to make mud in church and then smeared it all over that mirror so you could still tell it was a mirror, but certainly could not see yourself in it.

Owen's message that week was powerful as he asked us to think about what we could do in our lives to clean things up. He said, "When sin exists in our lives we, ourselves, are not able to reflect the love of God, we're not able to reflect the image of God." He proceeded to wipe away a swath of mud to where we could see ourselves in the mirror again. We were challenged to think about what we may be able to remove from our lives so we can truly be the person God created us to be. I left feeling challenged yet knew there was more to the challenge that would come the following week.

The next Sunday had the prop from the previous week—the mud-smeared mirror—and a new prop as well, a three-foot by five-foot moveable whiteboard that sat in front of the congregation, slightly off to one side.

At the top of the board read the words, "What is old..." During his sermon and as a form of response, Owen offered us the opportunity to walk up to the board and write something about ourselves that we'd like to let go of, something that may be keeping us from being the best version of ourselves. I did not find myself up at the board, mainly because all I could think about was this book that I was writing for you. This activity my fellow church members were being asked to go through, this opportunity to cleanse themselves, to find a new way forward after leaving some muddy stuff behind was the message of this book you hold in your hands. Chapter 12 was being written right in front of me, and I had a front-row seat.

Life is messy. We create messes. We live through messes. In the chapters previous to this one, you've read about a number of these messes—grief, losing a child, divorce, unanswered prayers—yet Allison and I have worked hard to equip you with some perspective to wipe away that mess, to be cleansed so you can focus forward.

I sat in the front row and watched my fellow 519ers write on a white board what Allison and I have written about here. As I pondered the enormity and overall super-coolness of this epiphany and moment, I also pondered taking a picture of the board. I waited and waited and wondered and wondered if it was the right thing to do. I wanted to capture an image because it was very clear I was going to share the story of this day. After sufficient time had been given for us to write our notes, Owen started toward the board, and it quickly became clear that I was going to get the perfect picture, and I did. In it, you could see he had a spray bottle full of whiteboard cleaner in his hand and he was spraying the board to then wipe away "What is old." This, my friends, is what we aimed to do with this book. We have given our level best to give you a perspective that, when applied to your life experiences, will help you acknowledge your mess, move beyond it and identify the good—the message—that can result.

After cleaning the board, Owen offered us a new opportunity—to step up and write what we have done (or will do) in order to "...do a new thing" (Isaiah, 43:19), to reflect the image God created for us. This time, I was the first to the board to take Owen up on his offer, and I wrote, "Stop holding things in—start sharing my mess for the benefit of others." Those words, those actions, were the key to me surviving and thriving after two failed attempts at taking my own life. As you read earlier, when I was in high school—with no faith foundation, with no perspective that the black cloud of doom created by a bad breakup and materialism my family could not afford could possibly go away—I attempted suicide. Twice. After being given the gift of perspective that I mattered to many, that I was worthy of being on this planet and, most important to my recovery, that my experiences—my mess—could help others, I was given new life. Literally. We all have the ability to do the same; we just need to pick up the whiteboard cleaner and a marker.

Mess to message: *Thank you, Owen, for walking the congregation through a mess-to-message activity and for all you have done to help us love well and live differently where we live, work and play.*

† ORDINARY THINGS †

When did Owen first hear the calling from God to go into ministry? Did he resist God's nudge or quickly respond to His calling? How many people would have missed out on hearing the Gospel if Owen hadn't responded? Has he ever felt overwhelmed by the responsibility that God has given Him to share the Gospel or does he always keep in mind God is Master Planner?

My first book was a devotional called *The Whisper of God*. It was written around ordinary life events that happened to me, and I tied them back to the Bible. I used these everyday situations to illustrate how God spoke to my heart, encouraged me, provided and rebuked me through ordinary everyday things. The most significant part of these lessons always tied back to scripture. Just as John 14:21 says, **He will show Himself to those who keep His commands**, but it doesn't say He will do so in a cloud of fire, text message, Facebook© video or grand dream. One of the main ways God reveals Himself is through His written word—scripture!

I've encountered many people along my path through ministry and life. Many who will say they could never believe what the Bible says or that God is real. I always ask them if they have read the Bible. Interestingly, their answer on every occasion is no. Those who claim they could never believe usually haven't even read the Bible. Those who are waiting for some divine visitation to accept God, but have never opened the scriptures and looked for Him in the most reliable place. They have given up and formed an opinion before even examining the facts.

These children of God burden my heart. I deeply desire for them to know and experience God's unfathomable love, grace, and mercy. I wonder why it's so difficult for some to trust and believe in Him? Is it a broken relationship with their earthly father, difficult life circumstances they can't come to grip with, a fear of letting go of control or being loved wholeheartedly?

I'll never forget one of my first reviews on Amazon, "Sorry, but the inside content doesn't help you see God in the ordinary…" That stung a bit until I realized this reader was probably counting more on **me** to offer her direction than she was on the scriptures and God Himself. I promise that if you look at the "inside content" of <u>His</u> written word, God will never let you down. He will reveal Himself to you. You can read every Bible study written by someone who speaks to thousands or by me who only speaks to hundreds, and you will never see God revealed in the way you will if you focus on His written word.

The words of Bible study teachers, authors and commentators should only be a guide or an encouragement that lights the path to your face-to-face with God through His God-breathed Word.

Think about it this way, if you were coloring your hair for the first time, would you open the box, put the color on your hair and hope for the best without reading the instructions? Would you try to remember how your girlfriend told you to do it? Or would you sit and read each step before beginning? Hair is super-important to women, at least! I can't speak to men (especially not Scott) about this. I would probably read the directions six times before putting the first drop on my head. In the same way, how can we keep God's commands if we haven't read them? Jesus is way more important than hair—even if I do get too caught up in a bad hair day now and then.

I pray that no matter what person or study you are looking to as your guide, you will use it as a tool to open your eyes to God's Word and His glorious mysteries.

Scott and I have shared stories and revelations with you to lead to you a bigger picture. If you don't remember anything else from this book, please remember these final truths and hold tight to them.

This is how we are sure that we have come to know Him: by keeping His commands. The one who says, "I have come to know Him," yet doesn't keep His commands, is a liar, and the truth is not in him. But whoever keeps His word, truly in him the love of God is perfected. This is how we know we are in Him. 1 John 2:3-5 (HCSB)

1. Know and obey God's commands. To understand his commands, keep and follow them, we must read His word. When we know them, we experience the strength that leaning on them offers. My prayer is that we will all ask and trust in our Heavenly Father for the strength, discipline, and faith to follow Him.

So now, little children, remain in Him, so that when He appears we may have boldness and not be ashamed before Him at His coming. 1 John 2:28 (HCSB)

2. It's not about this world, but our eternal one. We can get so caught up in the "wants" we forget to focus on all our needs that are being met daily. If we remain in God through His word, we have a greater chance of

overcoming idols and taking the narrow gate that will lead us to Him.

Anyone who does not remain in Christ's teaching but goes beyond it does not have God. The one who remains in that teaching, this one has both the Father and the Son. 2 John 9 (HCSB)

3. If we desire eternal life with our Heavenly Father, we must believe in His Son Jesus, and when we know the Father, we must remain in His teaching. If we know the Father and turn away from Him, we are no better than those who never believed.

I've expressed in chapter after chapter how vital it is to study scripture and get to know God. Although we can't touch on that in depth in this book, I hope you will check out my Bible study called *In the Mi[God]dle: Keys to keeping God in the middle of all you think, do and say.* Not only does it show you, through scripture, how much God desires to be in the center of our lives, but also what it declares about His character, the attributes we gain by putting Him in the middle and how to study scripture on your own.

If all this is new to you, I pray you will seek out a godly friend or pastor who can answer more in-depth questions about following Jesus. However, if you have had it on your heart to accept Jesus Christ as your personal Savior, it is with great honor I share a simple prayer you can pray to receive Him into your heart today.

God, I know that, in my lifetime, I have not always lived for you, and I have sinned in ways I probably don't even know yet are sins. I know that you have plans for me, and I want to live in those plans. I pray to you for forgiveness for all the ways in which I have sinned.

I am choosing now to accept you, Jesus, into my heart. I am eternally grateful for your sacrifice on the cross and how you died so I can have eternal life. I pray that I will be filled with the Holy Spirit and that I continue to live as you desire for me to live. I will strive to overcome temptations and no longer let sin control me. I put myself--my life and my future--in your hands. I pray that you work in my life and guide my steps so that I continue to live for you for the rest of this life. In your name, I pray. Amen.[vii]

Thank you for taking this journey with us. I want to leave you with my favorite verses from Romans (MSG).

PRAYER
So here's what I want you to do, God helping you: Take your everyday, ordinary life—your sleeping, eating, going-to-work, and walking-around life—and place it before God as an offering. Embracing what God does for you is the best thing you can do for him. Don't become so well-adjusted to your culture that you fit into it without even thinking. Instead, fix your attention on God. You'll be changed from the inside out. Readily recognize what he wants from you, and quickly respond to it. Unlike the culture around you, always dragging you down to its level of immaturity, God brings the best out of you, develops well-formed maturity in you. Romans 12:1-2 (MSG)

CONCLUSION

*T*hen *he said, "Go into the world. Go everywhere and announce the Message of God's good news to one and all. Whoever believes and is baptized is saved; whoever refuses to believe is damned. Mark 16:15-16 (MSG)*

What a bold and clear directive!

As I've mentioned, one of my biggest discouragements is hearing people express that the Bible isn't relevant anymore. I'm passionate about the Word of God because Jesus was always a friend of a friend until I began to read the Bible and know His character, love, truths, and promises for my own. I quit listening to what everyone else said about Him and found out for myself. After that, He became my personal friend, and my prayer is that everyone will call Him that.

When God is a personal friend, we begin to see the message in all the mess. Even though this book is filled with the people from Scott's life that have made an impact on him, I believe that if you look closely at your own life, you will see God has put people in your life that have impacted you as well. Their stories are woven into yours and yours into theirs. This is the beauty of God's people. He takes us, and the mess we fall into or the mess we create and He somehow uses it for His glory and master plan.

The Bible is our face-to-face with God. It's a glorious love story full of epic battles, trials, triumphs, and mystery. In it, we are introduced to many people from Genesis to Revelations that were ordinary people with a pile of sins, mess, and confusion. The story ends up better for some than others, but those who overcame are the ones who leaned on, trusted and followed our extraordinary God.

I often wonder, "Why me God? There isn't anything special about me. I've messed up so much along the way. Isn't there someone who would be better at sharing your message than me?" And God whispers to my heart, "Allison, I don't need you to go out there and die on the cross. I've covered the hard part. I simply need you to go out there and share your story. The story of how I have worked in your life and how you have overcome challenges and trials to find joy and meaning. Can you do that?" Sure is hard to say no to that.

I hope that you will find encouragement through the scriptures and Biblical truth I've tied into each chapter. Being introduced to some of the flawed, but deeply loved, people God used throughout history to accomplish God's will can richly build up your faith, courage, and trust in the Lord. Even if you never have a book written about you, a building named after you or even a child following your lead, you are just as much a part of God's plan and story as everyone else who has come before you and will come after you. He is calling to you to step up and be His plan A. The question is, will you answer the call?

*

I am a disciple of the Messiah.
I will not let up, look back or slow down.

My past is redeemed, my future secure. I am done with low living,
small planning, smooth knees, mundane talking, chincy giving and dwarfed goals.

I no longer need pre-eminence, prosperity, position or
popularity.
I don't have to be right, tops, recognized, praised or rewarded.
My face is set; my goal is sure.

My road is narrow; my way is rough, my companions few.
My God is reliable; my mission is clear.

I cannot be bought, compromised, detoured, delayed or deluded.
I will not flinch in the face of adversity, not negotiate at the table
of
my enemy or meander in the maze of mediocrity.

I am a disciple of the Messiah.

I must go until He comes, speak of all I know of Him and work
until He stops me.
And when He comes for His own, by the grace of God, He will
have no problem
Recognizing me, because my colors are clear.

-Unknown Zimbabwean Pastor

Mess To Message

Scott's Resources

Dumb and Dumber, Peter & Bobby Farrelly, New Line Cinema, 1994, film
Linda Ellerbee, www.inspiremetoday.com

Allison's Resources

[i] The Invitation, Tony Stultzfus, 2015, Coach22 Bookstore LLC
[ii] Cloud, Henry & John Townsend, How People Grow, 2001, Zondervan: How People Grow reveals why all growth is spiritual growth and how you can grow in ways you never thought possible. Unpacking the practical and passionate theology that forms the backbone of their counseling, Drs. Henry Cloud and John Townsend shatter popular misconceptions about how God operates to reveal how growth really happens.
[iii] www.goodreads.com/quotes
[iv] https://www.stewardship.com/articles/3-things-the-bible-says-about-money
[v] https://emilymcdowell.com/
[vi] https://emilymcdowell.com
[vii] https://www.thoughtco.com/a-simple-salvation-prayer-712283 by Kelly Mahoney

CPSIA information can be obtained
at www.ICGtesting.com
Printed in the USA
LVHW080520290419
615915LV00031B/637/P